"Praise him with the trumpet and with lute and harp. tambourines and processional. Praise him with stringed instruments and horns. Praise him with the cymbals, yes, loud clanging cymbals. Let everything alive give praises to the Lord!"

Psalm 150:3-6 (TLB)*

500 Hymns for Instruments

Arranged from the hymnal WORSHIP IN SONG
By Harold Lane

Book C
　　VIOLINS I, II, III
　　FLUTES

Lillenas Publishing Co.
KANSAS CITY, MO. 64141

500 HYMNS FOR INSTRUMENTS is designed as an accessory to the Lillenas hymnal, *Worship in Song*. The two books are identical in matters of numerical sequence, key, meter, and tempo indications. The harmonic structure is also basically the same with only slight variations. In *500 Hymns for Instruments*, an occasional passing chord has been inserted between syllables of the hymn or as a pickup to the refrain. Infrequently, an additional chord tone (a 7th, for example), not part of the hymnal harmony, has been inserted. These variations are to complement the harmony in the hymnal and not to clash with it.

The instrumentation is useful with many other current evangelical hymnbooks, for the harmonizations of most hymns and gospel songs are fairly uniform. The chord symbols in Book F are useful for comparing harmony. Keys must be checked, and in a few instances keyboard instruments playing from a different hymnal may need to transpose.

Some criteria for this project were that individual instruments have authentic parts suited to their unique capabilities; that these arrangements be performable by the various instrumental combinations in local situations; and that there be melody lines available in all possible keys and ranges so that every instrument would have solo possibilities.

These instrumentations will serve predominantly as accompaniment to congregational singing, but by design they are useful in a number of ways: for orchestra or smaller ensemble preludes, offertories, postludes, etc. An understanding of the organization of parts should make this versatility apparent:

For Solo (melody) →	**Trumpet I** **Violin I** **Trombone II**	**Horns (F) II** *(unless noted otherwise)* **Alto Saxophone I** **Rhythm**	
For Duet (add) →	**Trumpet II** **Violin II** **Trombone I**	**Horns (F) I** *(unless noted otherwise)* **Alto Saxophone II**	
For Trio (add) →	**Trumpet III**	**Violin III** **Trombone III**	
Countermelody →	**Tenor Saxophone**	**Baritone Treble Clef**	
Filler →	**Clarinets**	**Flutes**	
Bass →	**Bass Clarinet** **Tuba**	**String Bass** **Bass Guitar**	
Rhythm →	**Chord symbols**	**Drums**	

Combinations of instruments from any of the above groups may be made to work. Instruments playing in the same key can also alternate parts. For example, B-flat Clarinets can play B-flat Trumpet music. *Instrumental Handbook*, by Harold Pottenger (Beacon Hill Music, Kansas City, Mo.), is a useful guide to these possibilities.

French Horn parts are written for the F instrument. Also, the String Bass must be played *pizzicato* unless marked *arco* (with the bow).

1 How Firm a Foundation

Early American Melody

2 Joyful, Joyful, We Adore Thee

Arr. from Ludwig van Beethoven

3   To God Be the Glory   W. H. Doane

4   A Mighty Fortress Is Our God   Martin Luther

5   **How Great Thou Art!**

Swedish Folk Melody

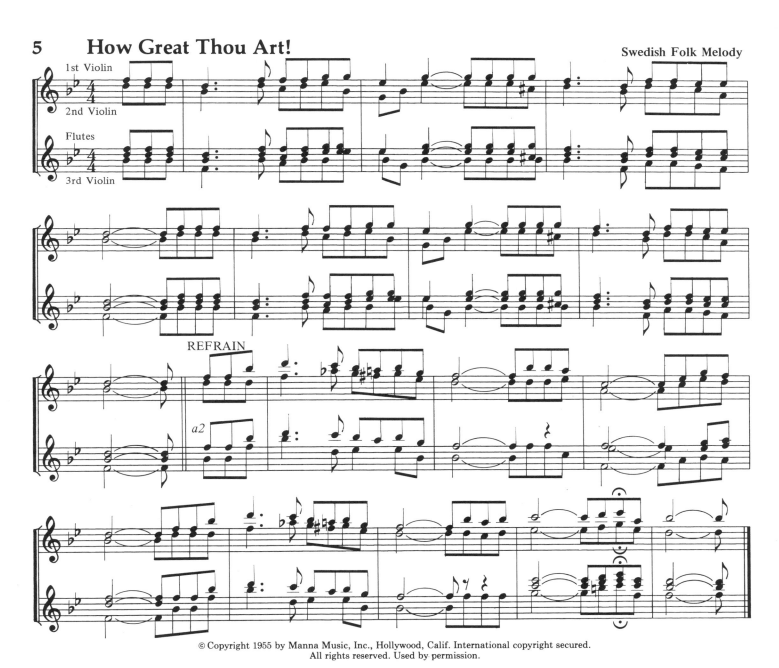

6   O Worship the King

Johann Michael Haydn

7   Majestic Sweetness

Thomas Hastings

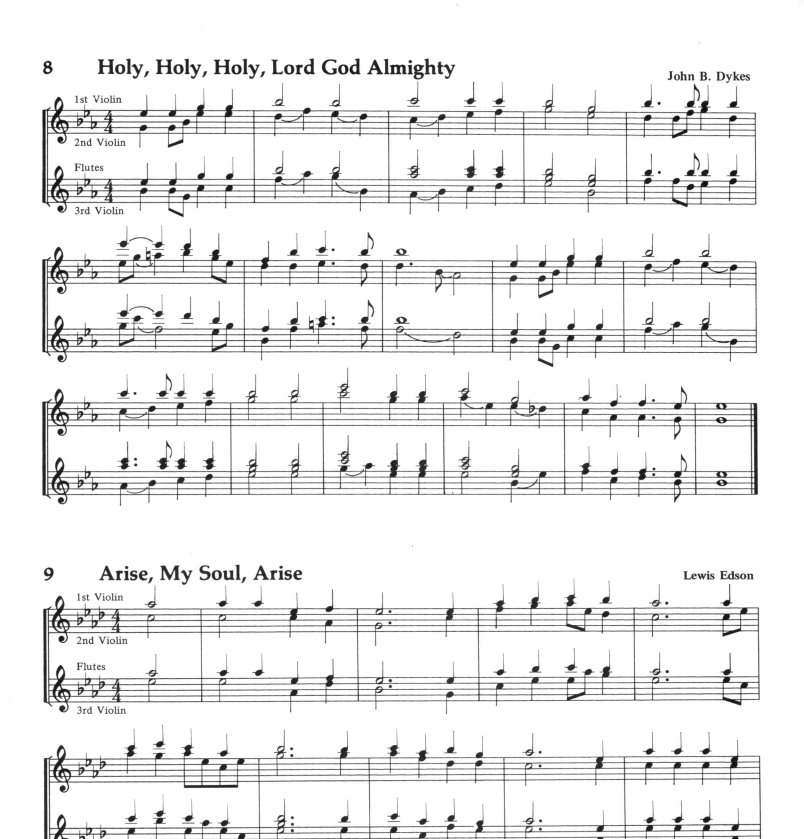

8 **Holy, Holy, Holy, Lord God Almighty**

John B. Dykes

1st Violin

2nd Violin

Flutes

3rd Violin

9 **Arise, My Soul, Arise**

Lewis Edson

1st Violin

2nd Violin

Flutes

3rd Violin

10 **All Hail the Power of Jesus' Name**

James Ellor

11 **All Hail the Power of Jesus' Name**

Oliver Holden

12   O for a Thousand Tongues!

Carl G. Glazer

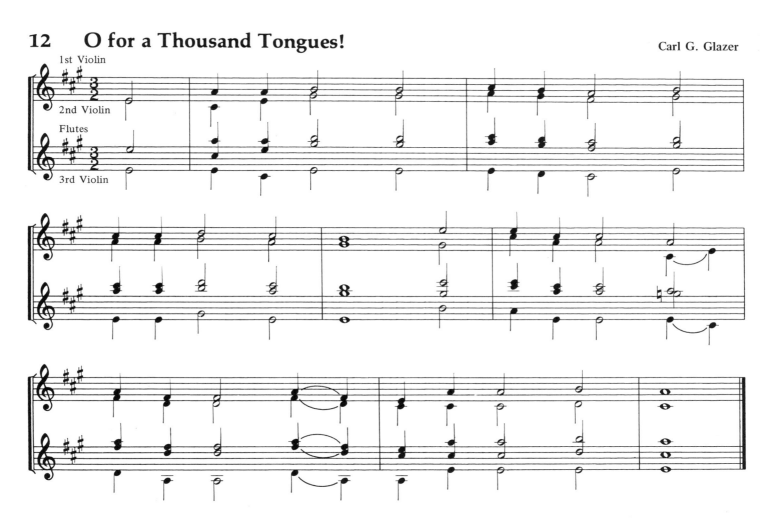

13   O Thou in Whose Presence

Freeman Lewis

14   O God, Our Help in Ages Past

William Croft

15 There's a Wideness

Lizzie S. Tourjee

16 Love Divine, All Loves Excelling

John Zundel

17 All Creatures of Our God and King

Melody from
Geistliche Kirchengesäng

18 This Is My Father's World

Franklin L. Sheppard

19   All Glory, Laud, and Honor

Melchior Teschner

20 **Eternal Father, Strong to Save**

John B. Dykes

21 **Come, Thou Almighty King**

Felice de Giardini

22 God Moves in a Mysterious Way

From Greatorex's "Collection"

1st Violin

2nd Violin

Flutes

3rd Violin

23 Jesus Shall Reign

John Hatton

24 Safely Through Another Week

Lowell Mason

25 Heavenly Father, King Eternal

L. Harold Johnston

26 For the Beauty of the Earth

Conrad Kocher

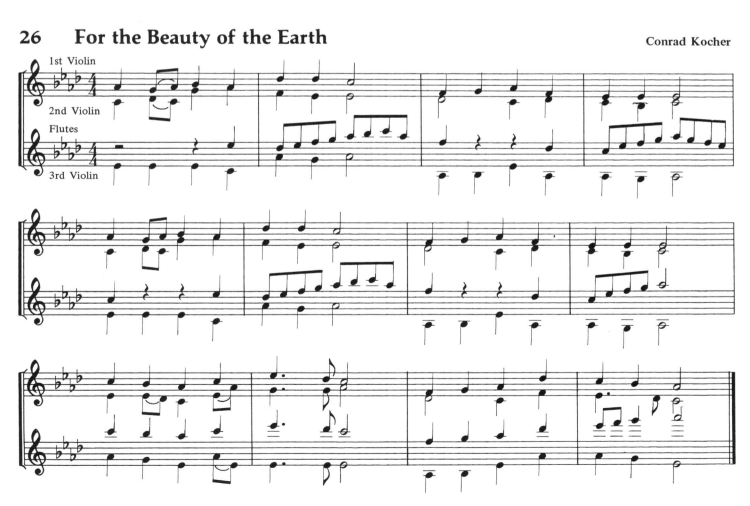

27 Sun of My Soul

From *Katholisches Gesangbuch*

28 Lead On, O King Eternal

Henry Smart

29 Immortal, Invisible

Welch Melody

30 God of Our Fathers

George W. Warren

31 O Could I Speak

From Arr. by Lowell Mason

32   Nearer, My God, to Thee

Lowell Mason

33 Take Time to Be Holy

George C. Stebbins

34 My Soul, Be on Thy Guard

Lowell Mason

35 O Love That Wilt Not Let Me Go

Albert L. Peace

36 Open My Eyes, That I May See

Clara H. Scott

37 **Jesus, Lover of My Soul**

Simeon B. Marsh

38 **A Closer Walk with Thee**

Haldor Lillenas

39 More Love to Thee

William H. Doane

40 I Want to Be like Jesus

David Livingstone Ives

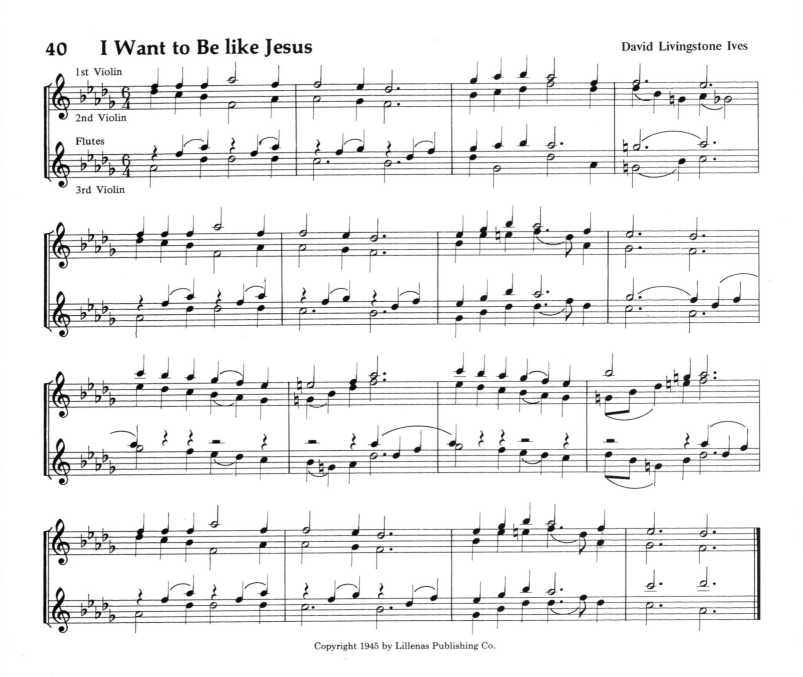

41 Be Still, My Soul

Jean Sibelius

42   Close to Thee

Silas J. Vail

43   O Master, Let Me Walk with Thee

H. Percy Smith

44   My Jesus, I Love Thee

Adoniram J. Gordon

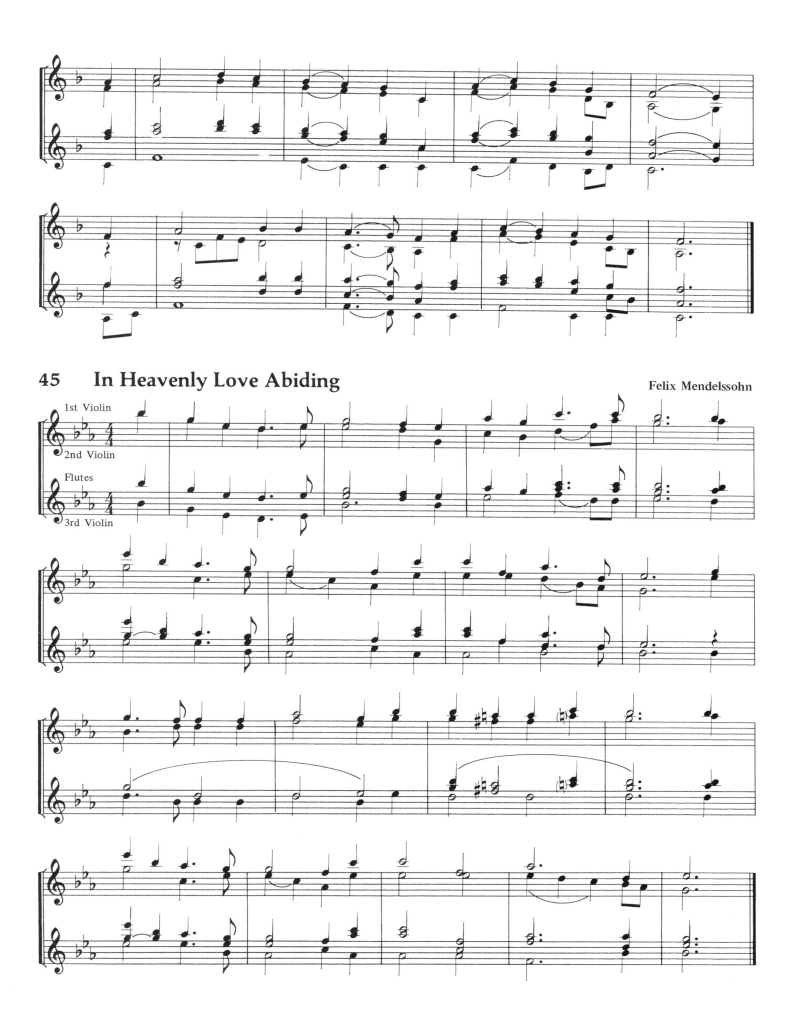

45   In Heavenly Love Abiding

Felix Mendelssohn

1st Violin

2nd Violin

Flutes

3rd Violin

46 He Hideth My Soul

William J. Kirkpatrick

Refrain

47 Rock of Ages

Thomas Hastings

48 Immortal Love, Forever Full

William V. Wallace

49 Abide with Me

William H. Monk

50 I Would Be like Jesus

Bentley D. Ackley

Refrain

51 In the Garden

C. Austin Miles

52   Unsearchable Riches

John R. Sweney

1st Violin

2nd Violin

Flutes

3rd Violin

Fine

Refrain

D.S. al Fine

53 O Jesus, I Have Promised

Arthur H. Mann

54 My Faith Looks Up to Thee

Lowell Mason

55 Come, Holy Ghost, Our Hearts Inspire

From *Este's Psalter*, 1592

56 Something for Jesus

Robert Lowry

57 **Trust in the Lord**

Wendell P. Loveless

1st Violin

2nd Violin

Flutes

3rd Violin

Refrain

58 **I Lay My Sins on Jesus**

Justin H. Knecht and
Edward Husband

1st Violin

2nd Violin

Flutes

3rd Violin

59   I Heard the Voice of Jesus Say

Old English Air

1st Violin

2nd Violin

Flutes

3rd Violin

Fine

D.C. al Fine

60   Sitting at the Feet of Jesus

Asa Hull

1st Violin

2nd Violin

Flutes

3rd Violin

Fine

61 Day by Day

Oskar Ahnfelt

62 Come, Thou Fount

John Wyeth

63 I Am Thine, O Lord

William H. Doane

64 Guide Me, O Thou Great Jehovah

Welch Hymn Melody
John Hughes

65 Guide Me, O Thou Great Jehovah

Thomas Hastings

66 Forever Here My Rest Shall Be

Hugh Wilson

67 Nearer, Still Nearer

Lelia N. Morris

68   O to Be like Thee

William J. Kirkpatrick

69 The Closer I Walk

Haldor Lillenas

70 It Is Well with My Soul

Philip P. Bliss

71   I Will Sing of My Redeemer

James McGranahan

72 I Will Praise Him

Margaret J. Harris

73 Praise Ye the Lord, the Almighty

Stralsund Gesangbuch
From *Praxis Pietatis Melica*

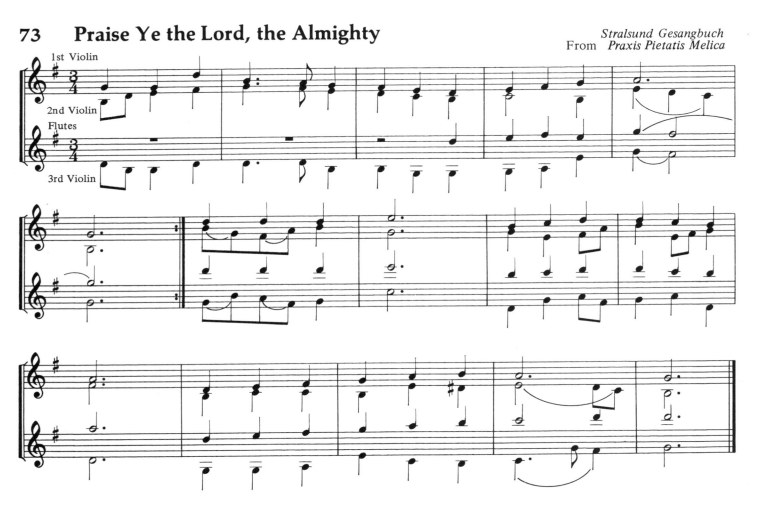

Let All the People Praise Thee

Lelia N. Morris

1st Violin

2nd Violin

Flutes

3rd Violin

Refrain

75 Come, We That Love the Lord

Aaron Williams

76 I Will Sing the Wondrous Story

Peter P. Bilhorn

77 Rejoice, the Lord Is King

John Darwall

78 **Praise Him! Praise Him!**

Chester G. Allen

79 Hallelujah! Amen!

Source Unknown

Refrain

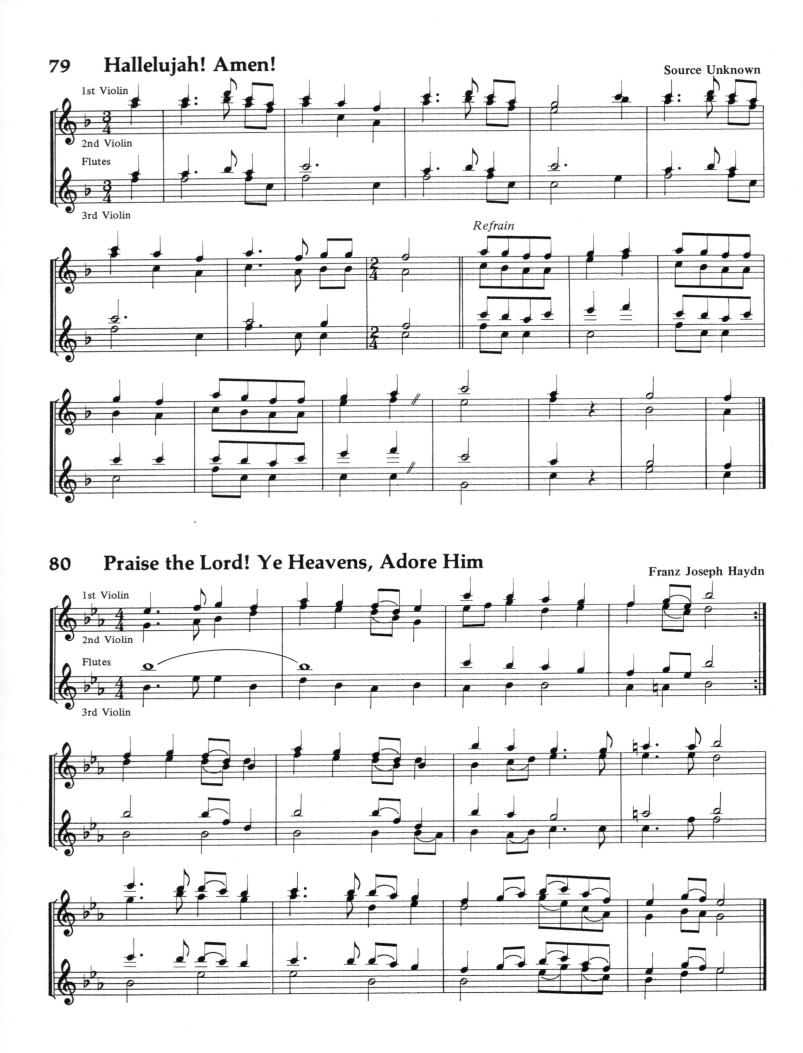

80 Praise the Lord! Ye Heavens, Adore Him

Franz Joseph Haydn

81 Glory to His Name

John H. Stockton

82 Rejoice, Ye Pure in Heart

Arthur M. Messiter

83 O for a Heart to Praise My God

Carl G. Gläser

84 Blessed Be the Name

Ralph E. Hudson

85 We Gather Together

Arr. from Netherlands Folk Song

86 Great Is Thy Faithfulness

William M. Runyan

87   Come, Ye Thankful People, Come

George J. Elvey

88   Now Thank We All Our God

Johann Crüger

89   Count Your Blessings

Edwin O. Excell

90 Break Thou the Bread of Life

William F. Sherwin

91 O Word of God Incarnate

Meiningisches Gesangbuch

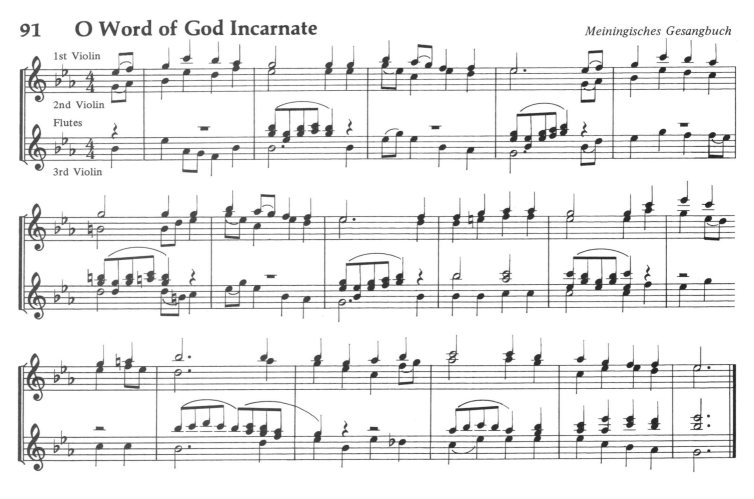

92   The Solid Rock

William B. Bradbury

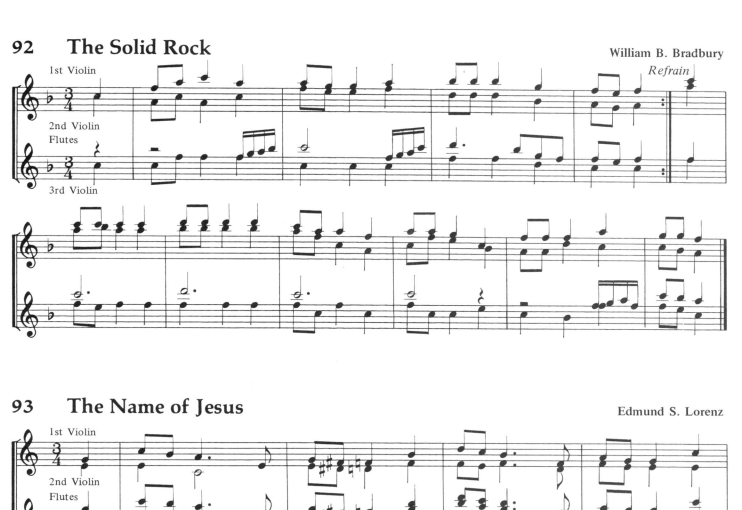

93   The Name of Jesus

Edmund S. Lorenz

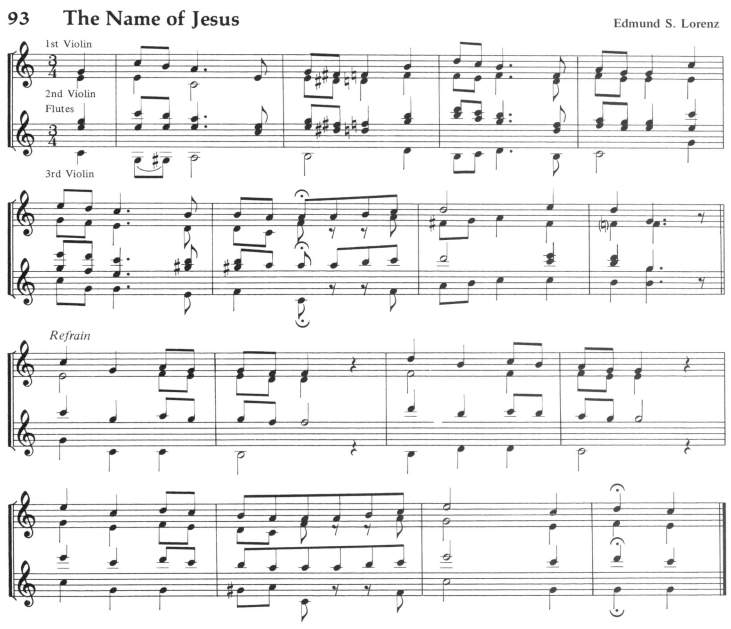

94 All That Thrills My Soul

Thoro Harris

95 Sweeter than All

J. Howard Entwisle

96 **The Light of the World Is Jesus**

Philip P. Bliss

97 The Unveiled Christ

N. B. Herrell

98 Our Great Saviour

Rowland W. Pritchard

99 Fairest Lord Jesus

From *Schlesische Volkslieder*

1st Violin

2nd Violin

Flutes

3rd Violin

100 Jesus, the Very Thought of Thee

John B. Dykes

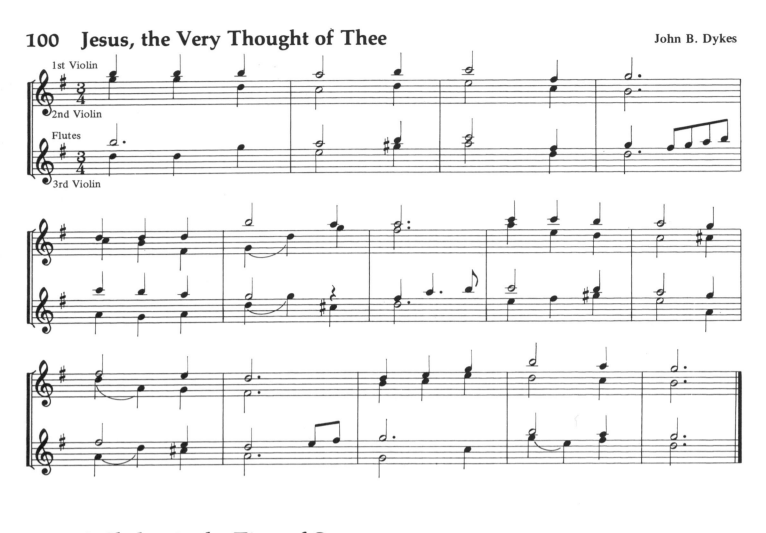

101 A Shelter in the Time of Storm

Ira D. Sankey

102 Jesus Is the Sweetest Name I Know

Lela Long

1st Violin

2nd Violin

Flutes

3rd Violin

Refrain

rall.

103 My Wonderful Lord

Haldor Lillenas

104 Blessed Redeemer

Harry Dixon Loes

105 Wonderful Saviour

J. M. Harris

106 The Great Physician

John H. Stockton

107 Altogether Lovely

Haldor Lillenas

108 All the Way Along

Lewis E. Jones

109 Take the Name of Jesus with You

William H. Doane

110 Jesus, Thou Joy of Loving Hearts

Source Unknown

111 How Sweet the Name of Jesus Sounds

Alexander R. Reinagle

112 My Jesus, as Thou Wilt

Carl M. von Weber

113 Give Me Jesus

John R. Sweney

114　What a Wonderful Saviour!

Elisha A. Hoffman

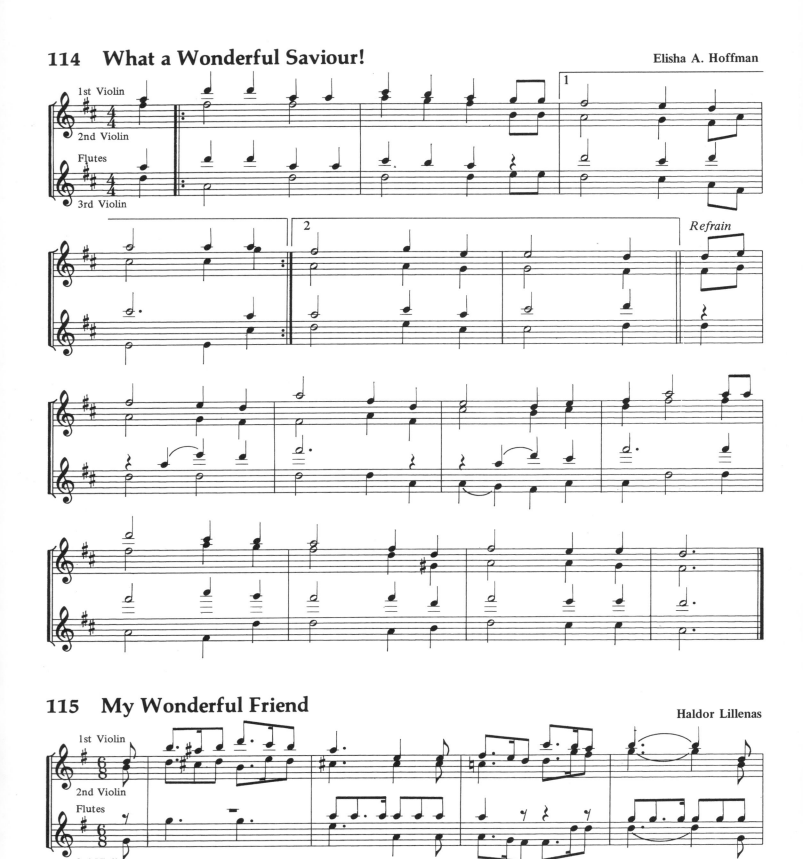

115　My Wonderful Friend

Haldor Lillenas

116 Tell Me the Stories of Jesus

Frederic A. Challinor

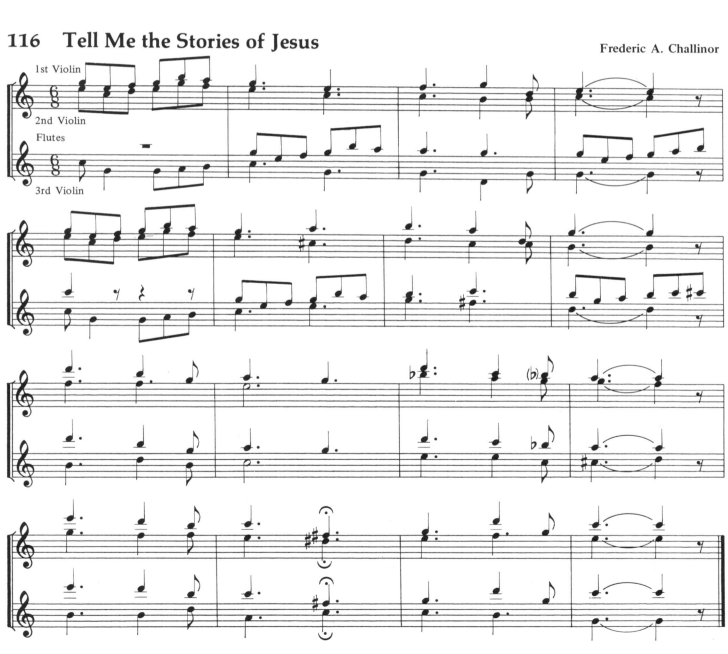

117 Why Do I Sing About Jesus?

Albert A. Ketchum

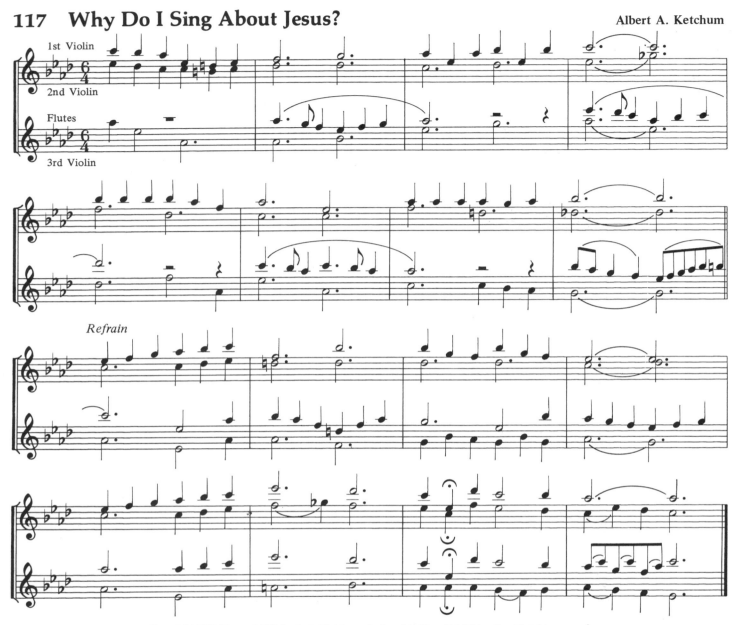

118 That Beautiful Name

Mabel Johnston Camp

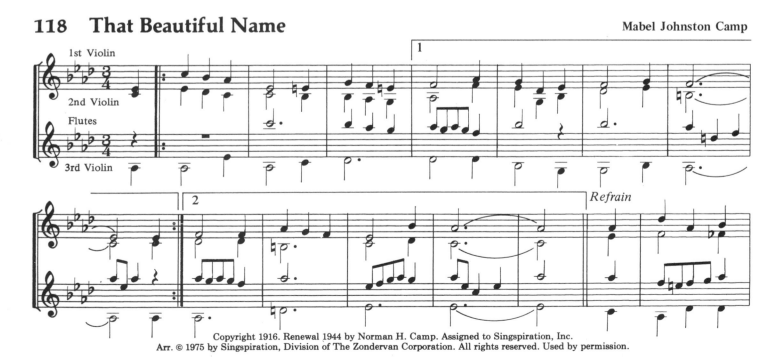

119   I Love to Walk with Jesus

Charles F. Weigle

120 Ride On! Ride On in Majesty

John B. Dykes

121 Wonderful

Alfred H. Ackley

122 More About Jesus

John R. Sweney

123 What a Friend We Have in Jesus

Charles C. Converse

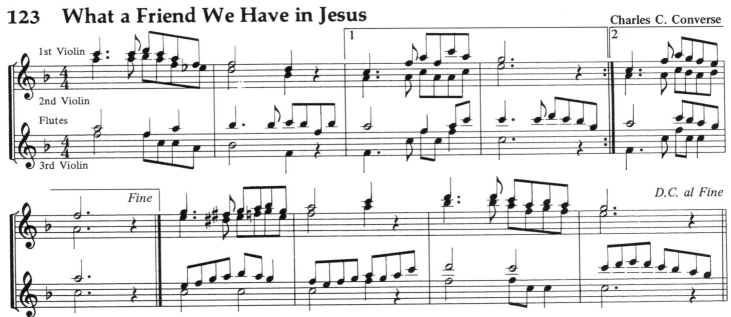

124 There Is a Fountain

Early American Melody

125 Blessed Be the Fountain

Henry S. Perkins

126 **Jesus, Thy Blood and Righteousness**

William H. Gladstone

127 Saved by the Blood

Bertha Mae Lillenas

128 He Loves Me

Anonymous

129 Covered by the Blood

Ran C. Story

130 Nothing but the Blood

Robert Lowry

131 When I See the Blood

John G. Foote

132 O Sacred Head, Now Wounded

Hans L. Hassler
Harm. by J. S. Bach

133 The Blood Will Never Lose Its Power

W. Stilman Martin

Refrain

134 It Cleanseth Me

A. F. Myers

135 Under the Atoning Blood

Haldor Lillenas

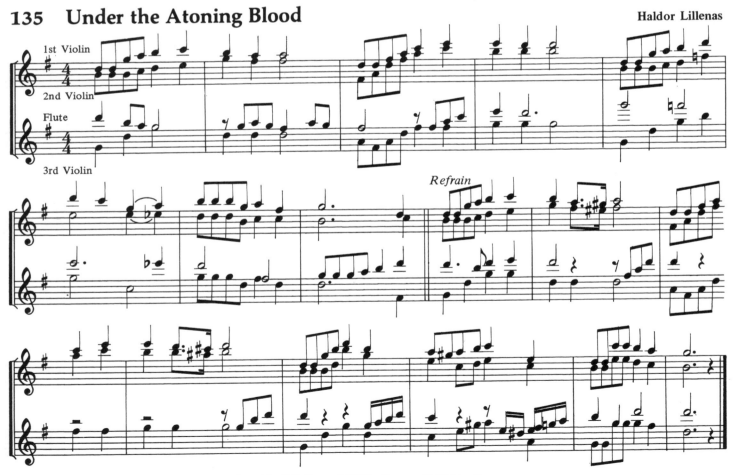

136 There Is Power in the Blood

Lewis E. Jones

137 Wounded for Me

W. G. Ovens

138 'Tis Midnight

William B. Bradbury

139 Near the Cross

William H. Doane

140 Lead Me to Calvary

William J. Kirkpatrick

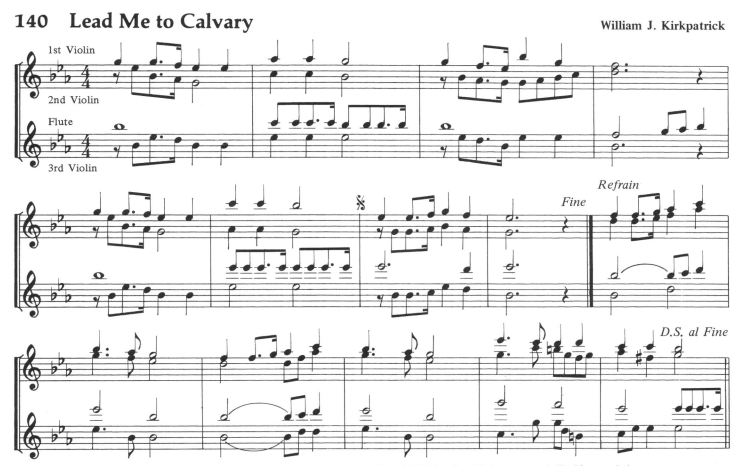

141 The Old Rugged Cross

George Bennard

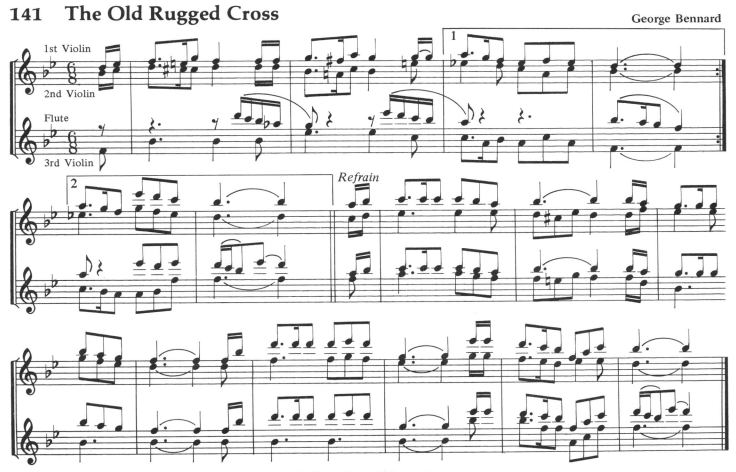

Hallelujah for the Cross

James McGranahan

1st Violin

2nd Violin

Flute

3rd Violin

Refrain

143 At the Cross

Ralph E. Hudson

144 When I Survey

From Lowell Mason

145 When I Survey

Isaac B. Woodbury

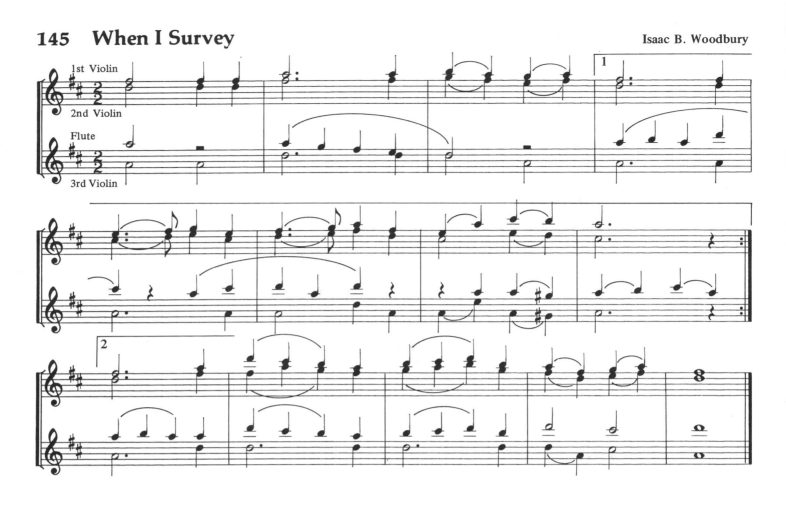

146 Must Jesus Bear the Cross Alone?

George N. Allen

147　In the Cross of Christ

Ithamar Conkey

148　There Is a Green Hill Far Away

George C. Stebbins

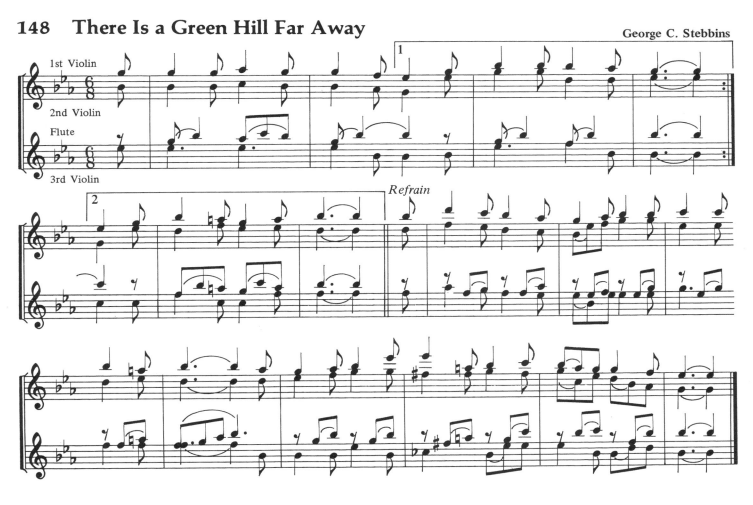

149   On the Cross of Calvary

Richard E. Gerig

1st Violin

2nd Violin

Flute

3rd Violin

150 The Way of the Cross Leads Home

Charles H. Gabriel

151 The Cross Is Not Greater

Ballington Booth

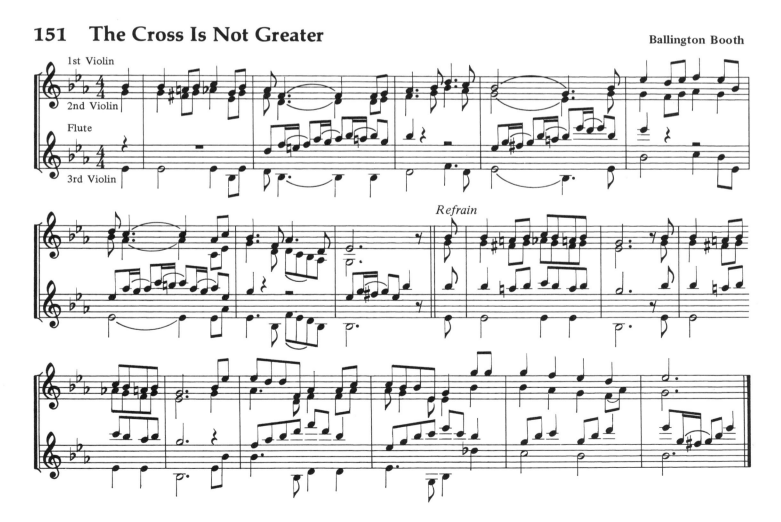

152 Beneath the Cross of Jesus

Frederick C. Maker

153 Calvary Covers It All

Mrs. Walter G. Taylor

154 Christ, the Lord, Is Risen Today

From *Lyra Davidica*

155 Christ Arose

Robert Lowry

156 I Know That My Redeemer Liveth

James H. Fillmore

157 The Lord Jehovah Reigns

John Darwall

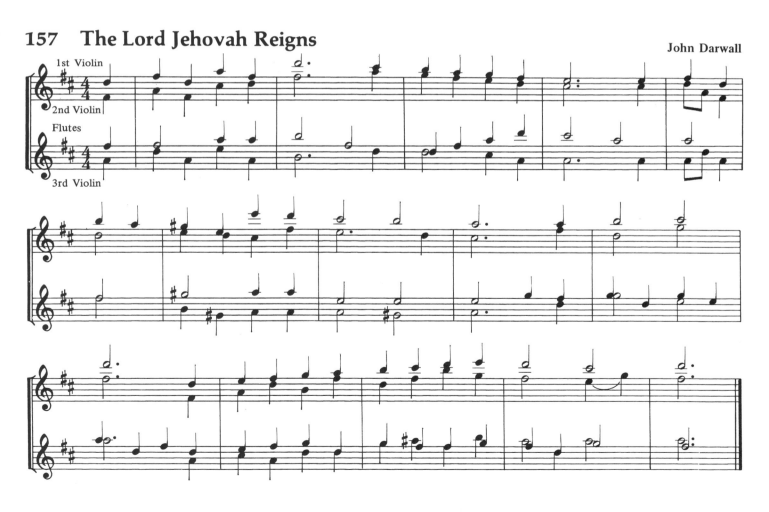

158 He Lives

Alfred H. Ackley

159 Why Should He Love Me So?

Robert Harkness

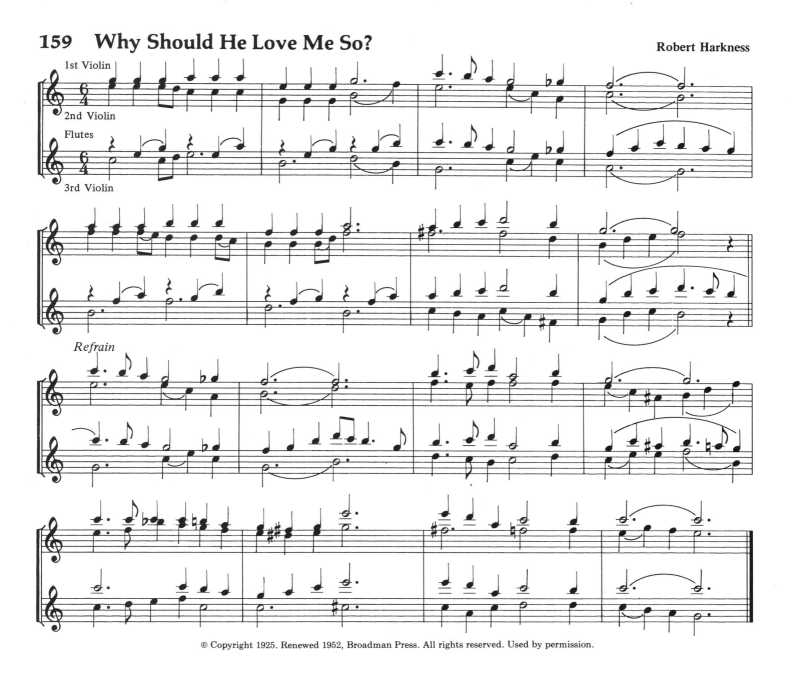

160 Hallelujah! What a Saviour!

Philip P. Bliss

161 Children of the Heavenly Father

Swedish Folk Melody

162 Crown Him with Many Crowns

George J. Elvey

163 Angels, from the Realms of Glory

Henry Smart

164 What Child Is This?

Old English Melody

165 Silent Night!

Franz Grüber

166 Hallelujah! Christ Is Born!

Faith Chambers Wilson

167 Thou Didst Leave Thy Throne

Timothy R. Matthews

168 Away in a Manger

John R. Murray

169 I Heard the Bells on Christmas Day

J. Baptiste Calkin

170 While Shepherds Watched Their Flocks

George F. Handel

171 O Come, O Come, Emmanuel

Plainsong, 13th Century

172 Joy to the World

George F. Handel

173 As with Gladness Men of Old

Conrad Kocher

174 O Little Town of Bethlehem

Lewis H. Redner

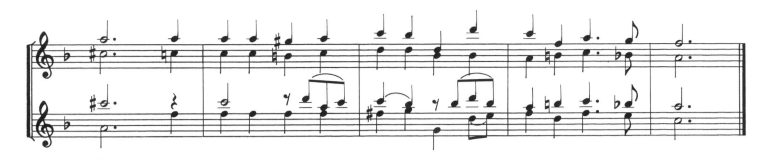

175   Hark! the Herald Angels Sing

Felix Mendelssohn

176 There's a Song in the Air

Karl P. Harrington

177 Good Christian Men, Rejoice

German Melody, 14th Century

178   O Come, All Ye Faithful

From Wade's *Cantus Diversi*, 18th Century

179 God Rest You Merry, Gentlemen

Traditional

1st Violin

2nd Violin

Flutes

3rd Violin

Refrain

180 Angels We Have Heard on High

French Carol

1st Violin

2nd Violin

Flutes

3rd Violin

181   Come, Thou Long-expected Jesus

Rowland H. Prichard

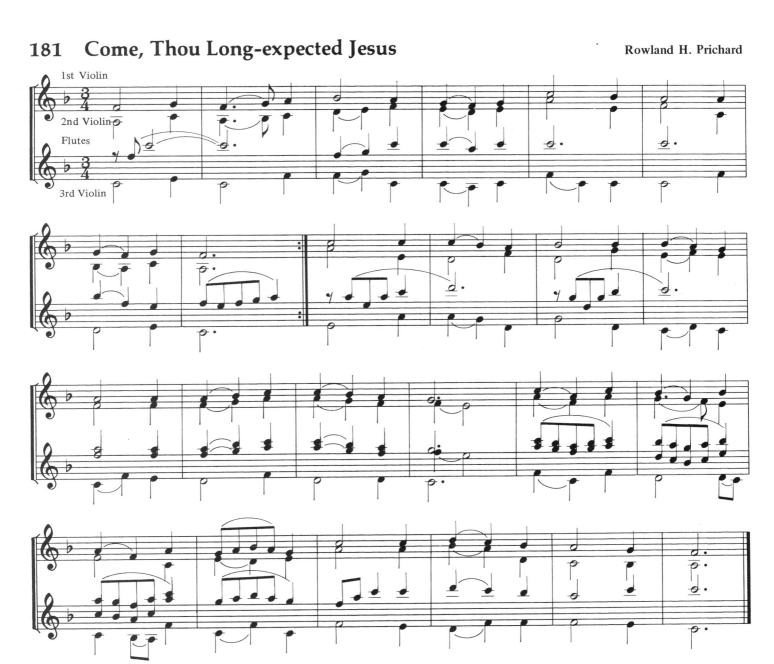

182 It Came upon the Midnight Clear

Richard S. Willis

183 The First Noel

Traditional Melody

184 Christ Returneth

James McGranahan

185 Jesus Is Coming Again

John W. Peterson

186 There's a Great Day Coming

Will L. Thompson

187 Will Jesus Find Us Watching?

William H. Doane

188 Is It the Crowning Day?

Charles H. Marsh

189 What if It Were Today?

Lelia N. Morris

190 **A Charge to Keep I Have**

Lowell Mason

191 Our Lord's Return to Earth Again

James M. Kirk

192 Lo! He Comes, with Clouds Descending

Henry T. Smart

(Instrumentation for No. 163 can be used if needed in B♭.)

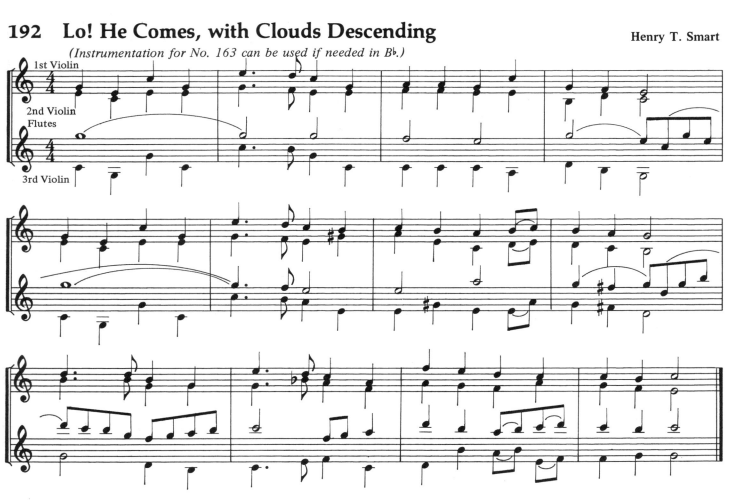

193 One Day

Charles H. Marsh

194 Am I a Soldier of the Cross?

Thomas A. Arne

195 **Tell Me the Old, Old Story**

William H. Doane

196 "Whosoever Will"

Philip P. Bliss

197 Christ Receiveth Sinful Men

James McGranahan

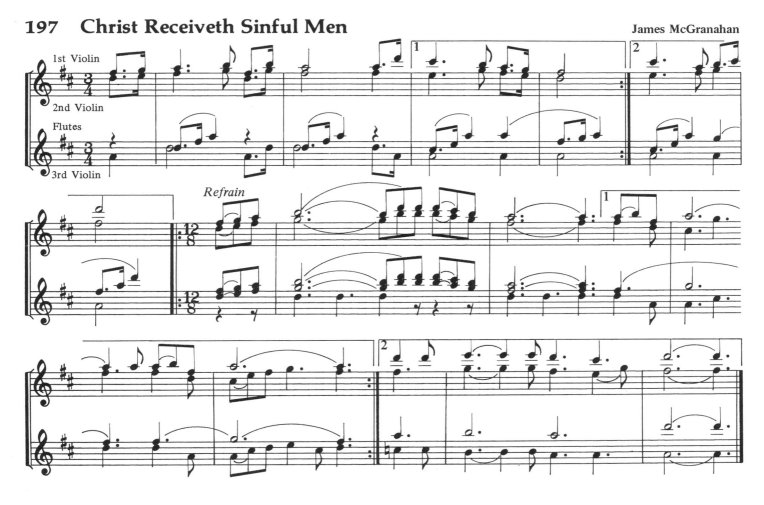

198 Jesus Saves

William J. Kirkpatrick

199 Look and Live

William A. Ogden

D.C. al Fine

200 Whosoever Meaneth Me

J. Edwin McConnell

1st Violin

2nd Violin

Flutes

3rd Violin

Refrain

201 'Tis Marvelous and Wonderful

Lelia N. Morris

202　And Can I Yet Delay!

Lowell Mason

203　Ho! Every One That Is Thirsty

Lucy J. Rider

204 Friendship with Jesus

Arr. from Stephen Foster

205 The Healing Waters

L. L. Pickett

206 Wonderful Words of Life

Philip P. Bliss

207 Turn Your Eyes upon Jesus

Helen H. Lemmel

1st Violin

2nd Violin

Flutes

3rd Violin

Refrain

208 Ye Must Be Born Again

George C. Stebbins

209 He Is Able to Deliver Thee

William A. Ogden

210 Mighty to Save

Ralph Schurman

1st Violin

2nd Violin

Flutes

3rd Violin

Refrain

211 The Song of the Soul Set Free

Alfred H. Ackley

1st Violin

2nd Violin

Flutes

3rd Violin

Refrain

212 Amazing Grace

Early American Melody

213 Grace Greater than Our Sin

Daniel B. Towner

214 Burdens Are Lifted at Calvary

John M. Moore

215 Wonderful Grace of Jesus

Haldor Lillenas

216 His Grace Is Enough for Me

J. Bruce Evans

217 His Grace Aboundeth More

William J. Kirkpatrick

218 **Wonderful Story of Love**

J. M. Driver

219   My Saviour's Love

Charles H. Gabriel

220   Such Love

Robert Harkness

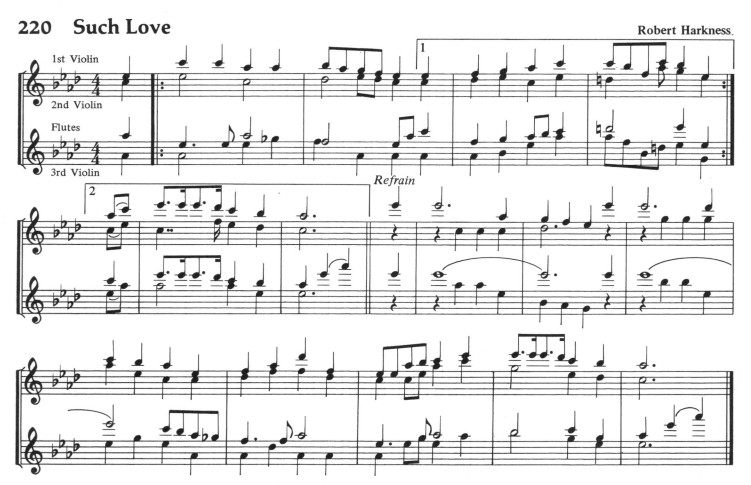

221 And Can It Be?

Thomas Campbell

222 Revive Us Again

John J. Husband

223 Spirit of the Living God

Daniel Iverson

224 **Send a Great Revival in My Soul**

B. B. McKinney

225 **There Shall Be Showers of Blessing**

James McGranahan

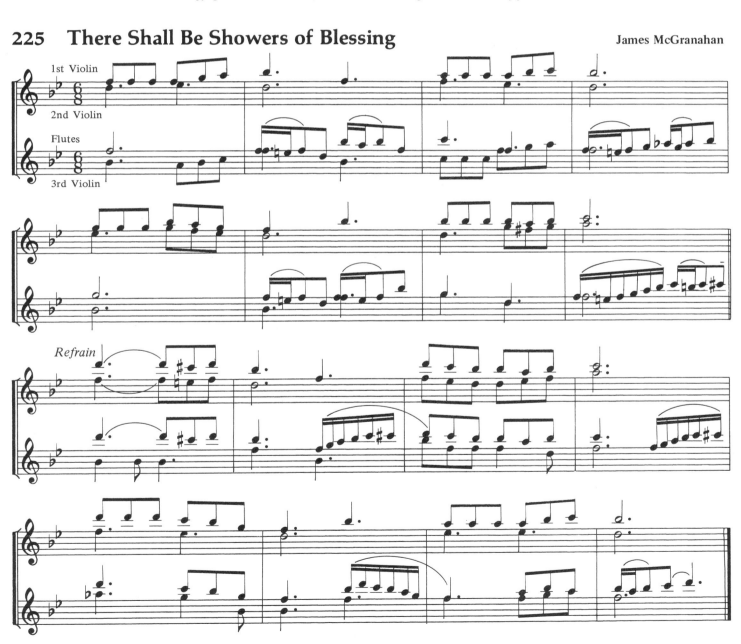

226 **Sweeping This Way**

Judson W. Van DeVenter
Arr. by Haldor Lillenas

227 **Jesus, I Come**

George C. Stebbins

228 Softly and Tenderly

Will L. Thompson

229 Let Jesus Come into Your Heart

Lelia N. Morris

230 Come Just as You Are

Haldor Lillenas

231 Pass Me Not

William H. Doane

232 Just as I Am

William B. Bradbury

233 Almost Persuaded

Philip P. Bliss

234 Give Me Thy Heart

William J. Kirkpatrick

235 The Saviour Is Waiting

Ralph Carmichael

236 Jesus Is Calling

George C. Stebbins

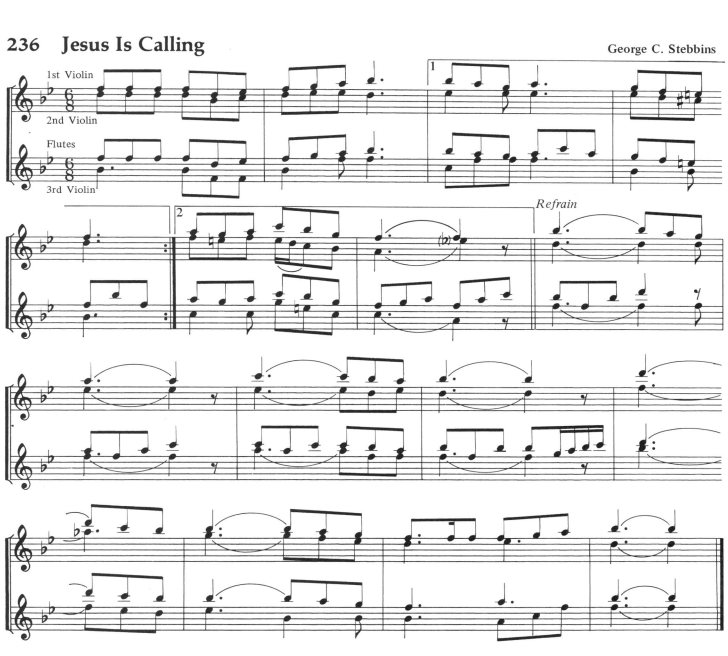

237 Don't Turn Him Away

Haldor Lillenas
Refrain Arranged

Refrain

238 For You I Am Praying

Ira D. Sankey

239 Room at the Cross for You

Ira F. Stanphill

240 You Must Open the Door

Homer A. Rodeheaver

241 His Way with Thee

Cyrus S. Nusbaum

242 Jesus Paid It All

John T. Grape

243 I'll Live for Him

C. R. Dunbar

244 I Do Believe

Unknown

245 Is My Name Written There?

Frank M. Davis

246 Is Thy Heart Right with God?

Elisha A. Hoffman

247 Only Trust Him

John H. Stockton

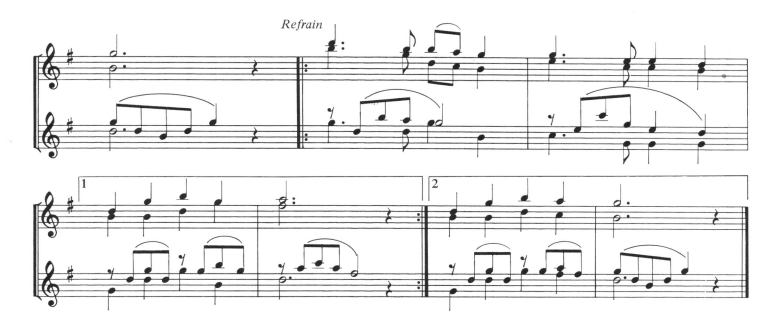

248 Wherever He Leads I'll Go

B. B. McKinney

249 Lord, I'm Coming Home

William J. Kirkpatrick

250 Are You Washed in the Blood?

Elisha A. Hoffman

251 I Am Coming, Lord

Lewis Hartsough

252 When We All Get to Heaven

Emily D. Wilson

253 My Saviour First of All

John R. Sweney

1st Violin
2nd Violin
Flutes
3rd Violin

Refrain

254 O That Will Be Glory

Charles H. Gabriel

1st Violin
2nd Violin
Flutes
3rd Violin

rit.

255 **Sweet By-and-by**

Joseph P. Webster

256 We Shall See the King Someday

Lewis E. Jones

257 When We See Christ

Esther Kerr Rusthoi

258   He the Pearly Gates Will Open

Elsie Ahlwen

259 When the Roll Is Called Up Yonder

James M. Black

1st Violin

2nd Violin

Flutes

3rd Violin

260 Saved by Grace

George C. Stebbins

1st Violin

2nd Violin

Flutes

3rd Violin

261 In the New Jerusalem

C. B. Widmeyer

262 From All That Dwell Below the Skies

John Hatton

263 Where They Need No Sun

Haldor Lillenas

264 Where Cross the Crowded Ways of Life

From **William Gardiner's** *Sacred Melodies*

265 Living Forever

Haldor Lillenas

266 Holy Ghost, with Light Divine

Louis M. Gottschalk

267 Spirit of God, Descend

Frederick C. Atkinson

268 Holy Spirit, Be My Guide

Mildred Cope

269 He Abides

D. M. Shanks

270 Fill Me Now

John R. Sweney

271 Bring Your Vessels, Not a Few

Lelia N. Morris

272 Breathe on Me

B. B. McKinney

REFRAIN

273 Pentecostal Power

Charles H. Gabriel

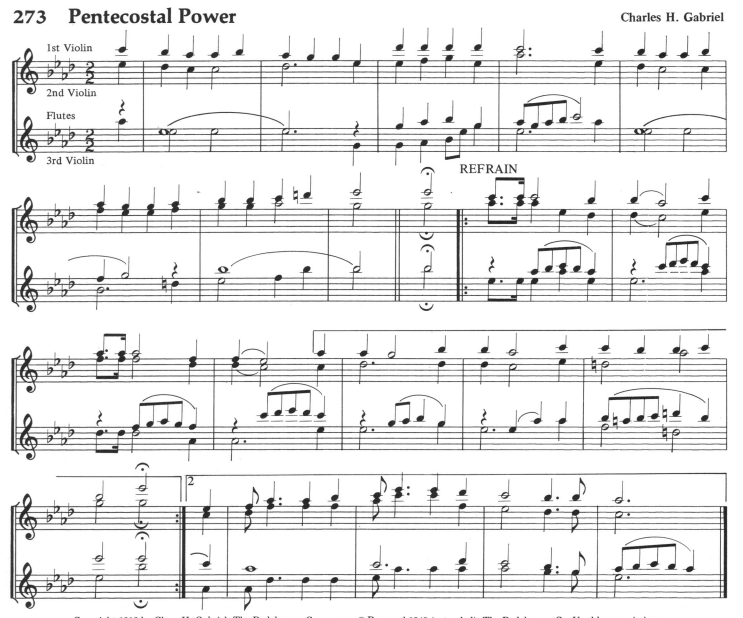

274 Since the Holy Ghost Abides

Mrs. F. E. Hill

275 The Comforter Has Come

William J. Kirkpatrick

276　Have Thine Own Way, Lord

George C. Stebbins

277　More like the Master

Charles H. Gabriel

278 Higher Ground

Charles H. Gabriel

279 Deeper, Deeper

Charles P. Jones

280 Is Your All on the Altar?

Elisha A. Hoffman

281 Take My Life, and Let It Be

Henri A. Cesar Malan

282 When Morning Gilds the Skies

Joseph Barnby

283 Dear Lord and Father of Mankind

Frederick C. Maker

284 I Gave My Life for Thee

Philip P. Bliss

285 Have Thy Way, Lord

George Bennard

286 Deeper and Deeper

Oswald J. Smith

287   I Surrender All

Winfield S. Weeden

288   Let Thy Mantle Fall on Me

Floyd W. Hawkins

289   Jesus, Thine All-victorious Love

Carl G. Glazer

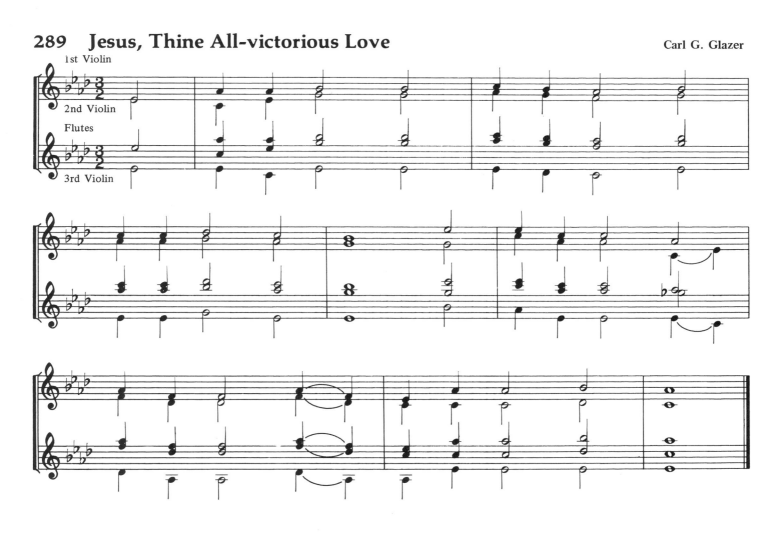

290 Holiness unto the Lord

Lelia N. Morris

291 All for Jesus

Asa Hull

292 Blessed Quietness

arr. from W. S. Marshall

293 The Glorious Hope

From Arr. by Lowell Mason

294 How the Fire Fell

Miriam E. Oatman

295 Holiness Forevermore

Haldor Lillenas

296 Sanctifying Power

Lelia N. Morris

297 Cleanse Me

Maori Melody

298 A Heart like Thine

Judson W. Van Deventer

299 Walking in the King's Highway

Florence Horton

300 The Cleansing Wave

Phoebe Palmer Knapp

301 Whiter than Snow

William G. Fischer

302 Since the Fullness of His Love Came In

Bentley D. Ackley

303 Breathe on Me, Breath of God

Robert Jackson

304 The Church's One Foundation

Samuel S. Wesley

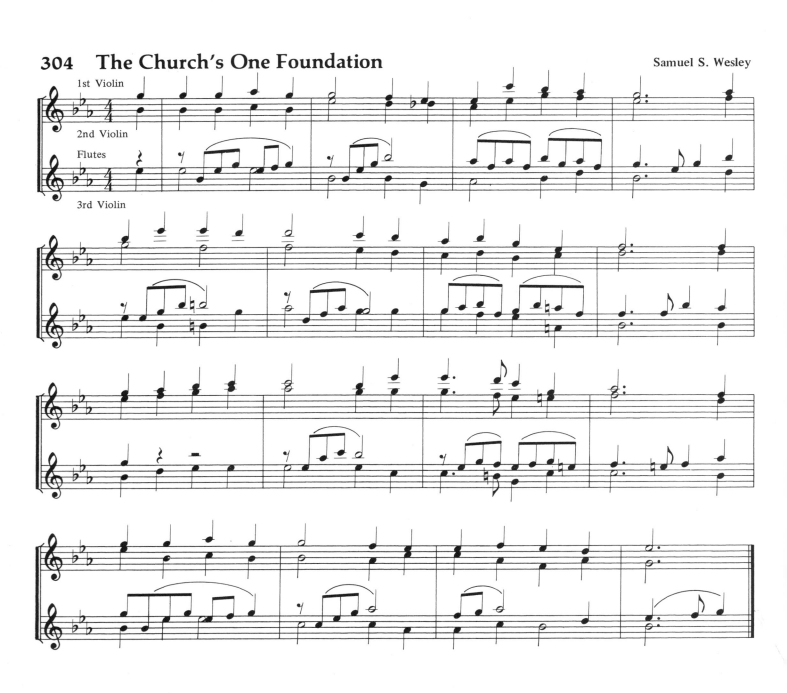

305 A Glorious Church

Ralph E. Hudson

306 In Christ There Is No East or West

Alexander R. Reinagle

307 Blest Be the Tie That Binds

From **Hans G. Nageli**
Arr. by Lowell Mason

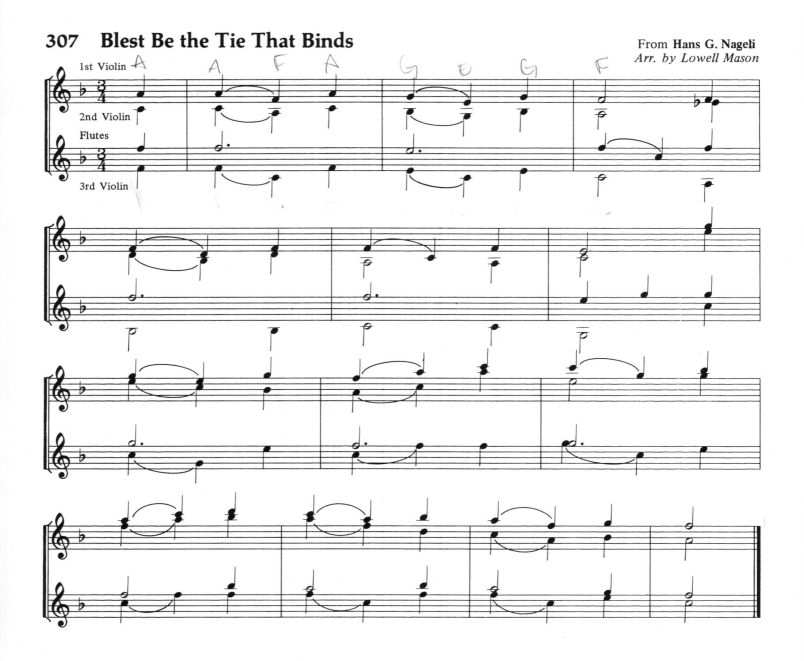

308 Glorious Things of Thee Are Spoken

Franz J. Haydn

*No. 80 may be used in key of E♭.

309 O Thou Whose Hand Hath Brought Us

Samuel S. Wesley

310 For All the Saints

Ralph Vaughan Williams

Tune from *The English Hymnal*. Used by permission of Oxford University Press, London.

311 I Love Thy Kingdom, Lord

Aaron Williams

312 Come, Holy Spirit, Heavenly Dove

John B. Dykes

313 According to Thy Gracious Word

From **Greatorex's "Collection"**

314   Bread of the World in Mercy Broken

John S. B. Hodges

315   Here at Thy Table, Lord

William F. Sherwin

316 Blest Feast of Love Divine

From **Hans G. Nageli**
Arr. by Lowell Mason

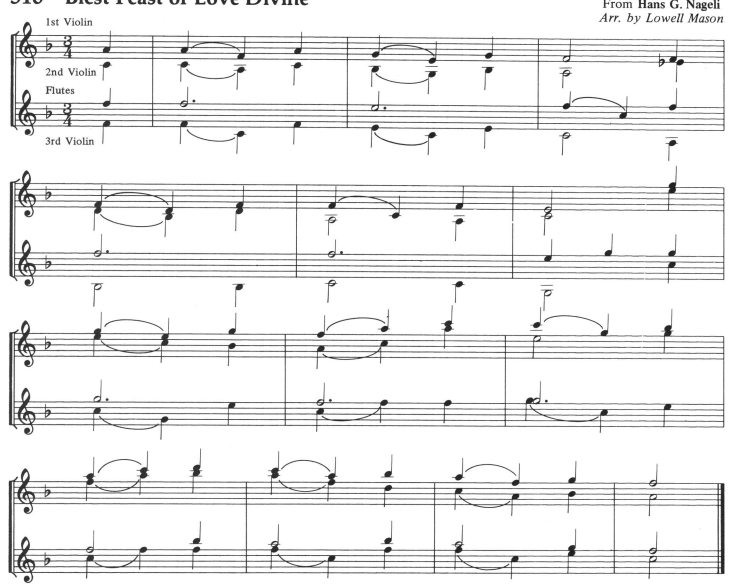

317 Let Us Break Bread Together

Traditional
Arr. by Floyd W. Hawkins

318 Who Is on the Lord's Side?

German Melody
Arr. by John Goss

319 Onward, Christian Soldiers

Arthur Sullivan

320 Stand Up for Jesus

George J. Webb

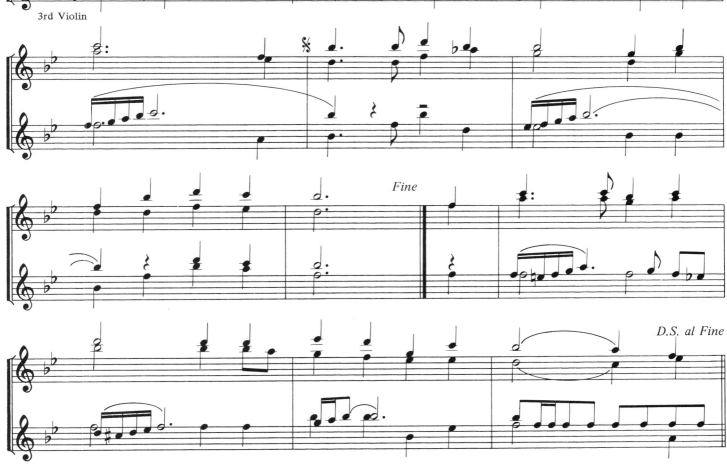

321 He Rolled the Sea Away

Henry L. Gilmour

322 Stand Up, Stand Up for Jesus

Adam Geibel

Refrain

323 Rise Up, O Men of God

William H. Walter

324 Sound the Battle Cry

William F. Sherwin

325 We're Marching to Zion

Robert Lowry

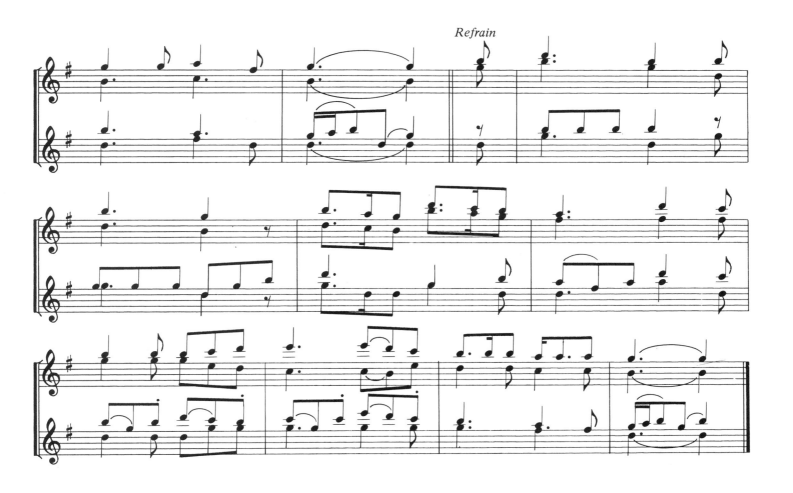

326 Jesus Calls Us

William H. Jude

327 Saviour, While My Heart Is Tender

George C. Stebbins

328 Follow On

Robert Lowry

329 Where He Leads I'll Follow

William A. Ogden

330 Anywhere with Jesus

Daniel B. Towner

331 Stepping in the Light

William J. Kirkpatrick

332 Follow, I Will Follow Thee

Howard L. Brown

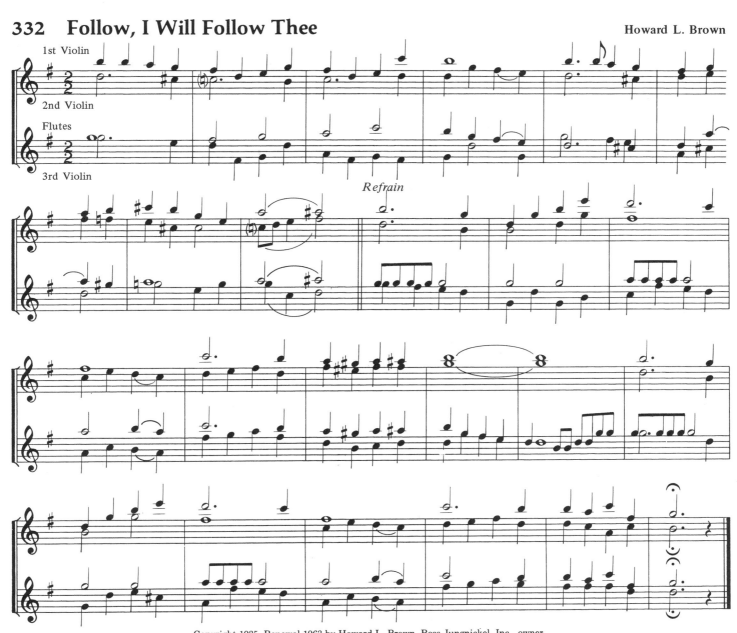

333 Living for Jesus

C. Harold Lowden

334 I Feel like Traveling On

Arr. by James D. Vaughan

335 Living for Jesus

Charles F. Weigle

336 To the Work

William H. Doane

337 Bring Them In

William A. Ogden

338 Lord, Speak to Me, That I May Speak

Robert Schumann

339 **Work, for the Night Is Coming**

Lowell Mason

340 **Give of Your Best to the Master**

Charlotte A. Barnard

341   I Do Not Ask to Choose My Path

Henry L. Gilmour

342 Make Me a Blessing

George S. Schuler

343 Ready

Charlie D. Tillman

344 In the Service of the King

Bentley D. Ackley

345 We'll Work till Jesus Comes

William Miller

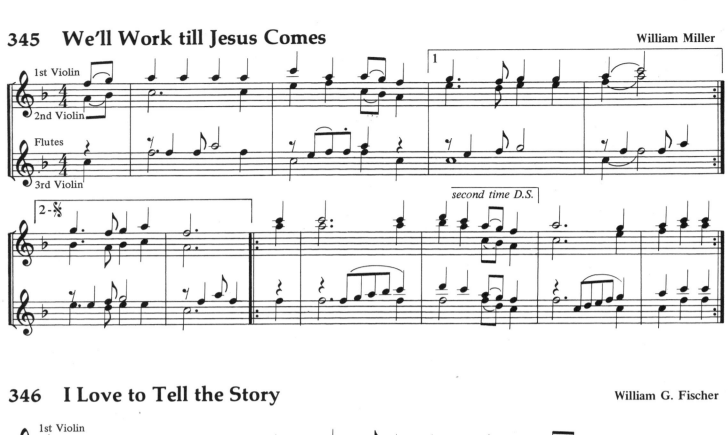

346 I Love to Tell the Story

William G. Fischer

347 We've a Story to Tell to the Nations

H. Ernest Nichol

348 The Call for Reapers

J. B. O. Clemm

349 Rescue the Perishing

William H. Doane

350 Tell the Blessed Story

Haldor Lillenas

351 Send the Light

Charles H. Gabriel

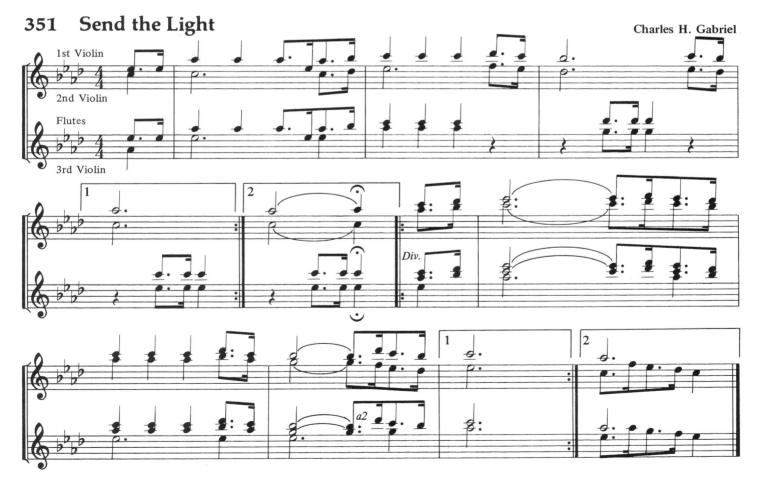

352 If Jesus Goes with Me

C. Austin Miles

353 The Morning Light Is Breaking

George J. Webb

354 I'll Go Where You Want Me to Go

Carrie E. Rounsefell

Refrain

355 Let the Lower Lights Be Burning

Philip P. Bliss

356 O Zion, Haste

James Walch

357 Redeemed

William J. Kirkpatrick

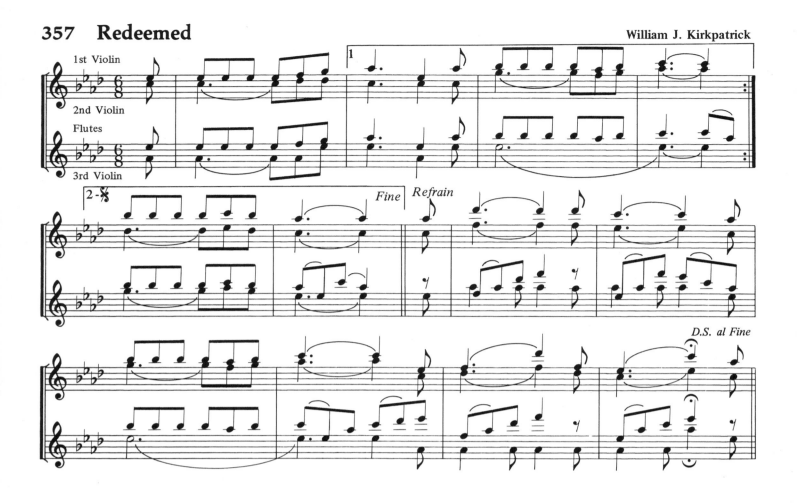

358 Hallelujah, I Am Free!

A. A. Jameson

359   I Love Him Better Every Day

Thoro Harris
Refrain by Adjt. Sidney Cox

360 He Is So Precious to Me

Charles H. Gabriel

361 Since I Have Been Redeemed

Edwin O. Excell

362 My Soul Is Filled with Glory

J. M. Harris

363 It is Truly Wonderful

Barney E. Warren

364 I Belong to the King

Maurice A. Clifton

365 Jesus Has Lifted Me

Haldor Lillenas

366 This Is like Heaven to Me

J. E. French

367 Jesus Is All the World to Me

Will L. Thompson

368 I've Found a Friend

George C. Stebbins

369 Then I Met Jesus

Byron M. Carmony

370 Springs of Living Water

John W. Peterson

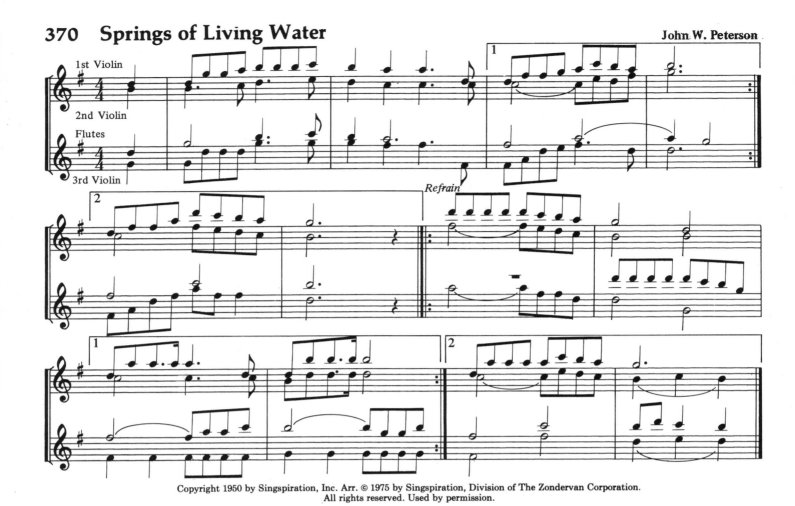

371 Still, Still with Thee

Felix Mendelssohn

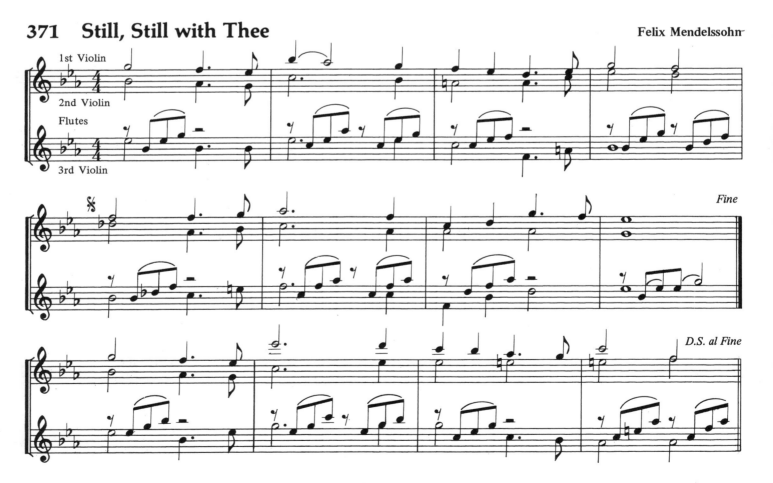

372 I Am Resolved

James H. Fillmore

373 Give Him the Glory

Elisha A. Hoffman

374 Sweeter as the Years Go By

Lelia N. Morris

375 He Lifted Me

Charles H. Gabriel

376 Heavenly Sunlight

George H. Cook

377 A Child of the King

Arr. by John B. Sumner

378 He Took My Sins Away

Margaret J. Harris

379   Saved to the Uttermost

William J. Kirkpatrick

380 It Is Mine

William Edie Marks

381 He Brought Me Out

Henry L. Gilmour

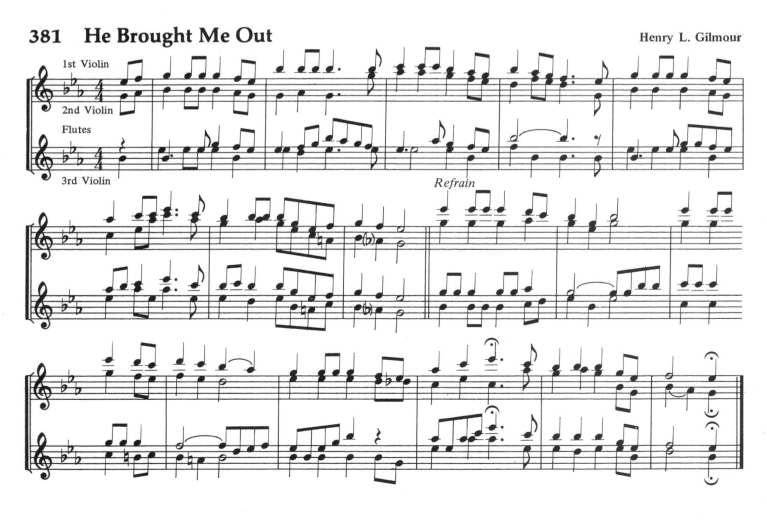

382 He Keeps Me Singing

Luther B. Bridgers

383 Saved, Saved!

Jack P. Schofield

384 Constantly Abiding

Anne S. Murphy

385 Jesus Is Mine

Theodore E. Perkins

Fine

D.S. al Fine

386 My Burden Is Gone

Haldor Lillenas

387 O How I Love Jesus

Traditional

388 My Burdens Rolled Away

Minnie A. Steele

389 My Sins Are Blotted Out, I Know!

Merrill Dunlop

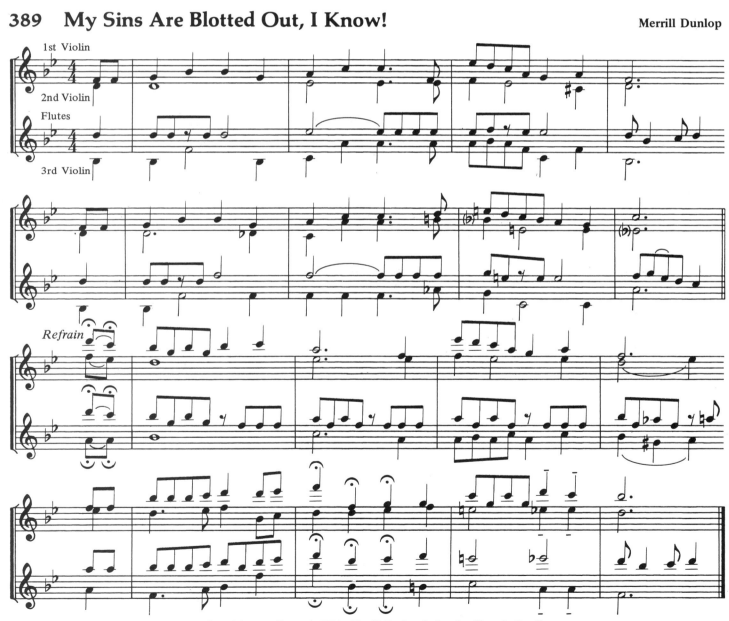

390 I've Anchored in Jesus

Lewis E. Jones

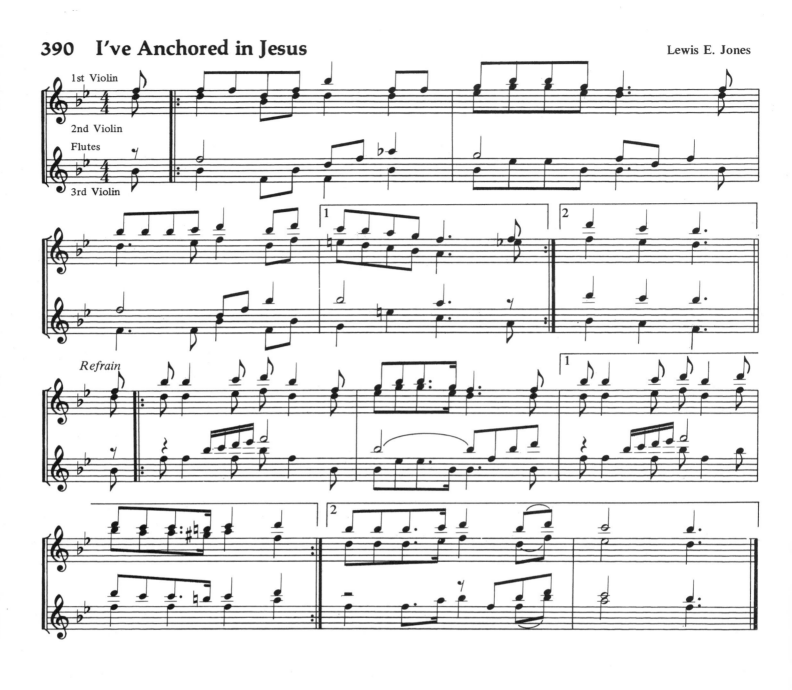

391 At Calvary

Daniel B. Towner

Refrain

392 Still Sweeter Every Day

C. Austin Miles

1st Violin

2nd Violin

Flutes

3rd Violin

Refrain

393 Where Jesus Is, 'Tis Heaven

James M. Black

394 The Crystal Fountain

Floyd Hawkins

395 Satisfied

Ralph E. Hudson

396 **He's Everything to Me**

Hampton H. Sewell

397 Where He Leads Me

John S. Norris

398 Jesus Is the Joy of Living

Alfred H. Ackley

399　O Happy Day

Edward F. Rimbault

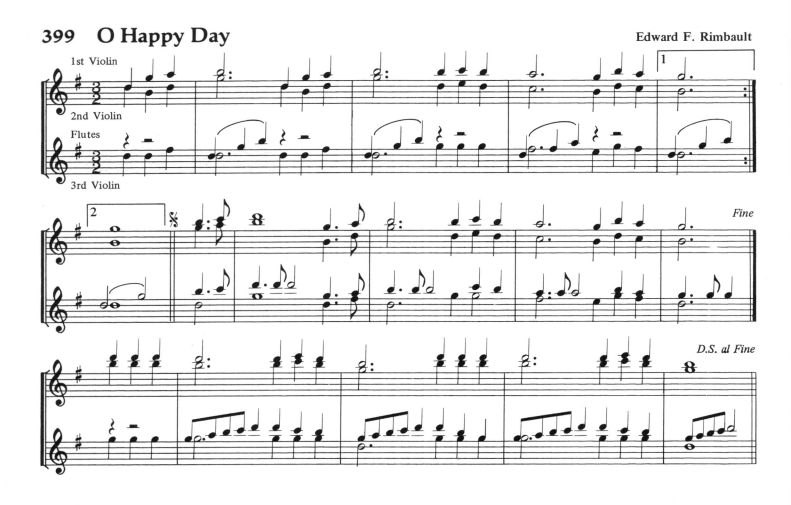

400　Love Lifted Me

Howard E. Smith

401 He's a Wonderful Saviour to Me

Blanche Kerr Brock

402 Since Jesus Came into My Heart

Charles H. Gabriel

403 I Know I Love Thee Better, Lord

Ralph E. Hudson

404   The Lily of the Valley

English Melody
William S. Hays

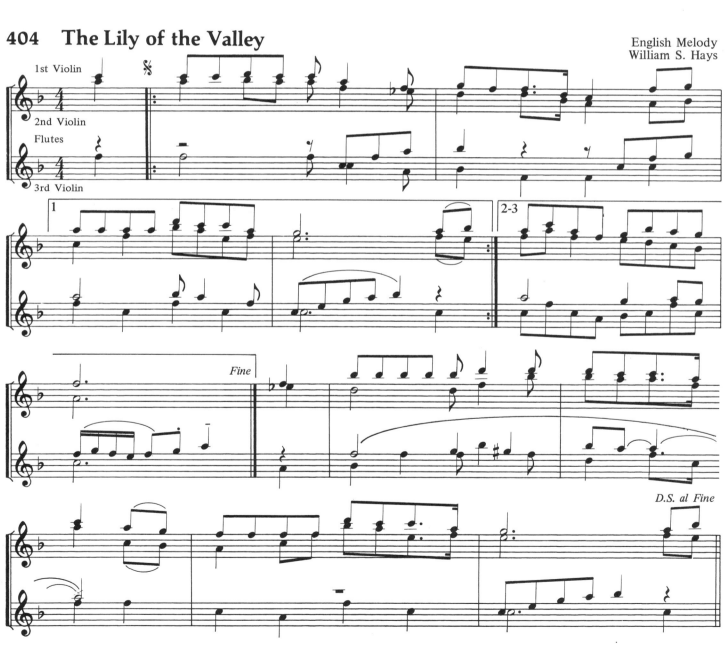

405 I'd Rather Have Jesus

George Beverly Shea

1st Violin

2nd Violin

Flutes

3rd Violin

406 Wonderful

Haldor Lillenas

1st Violin

2nd Violin

Flutes

3rd Violin

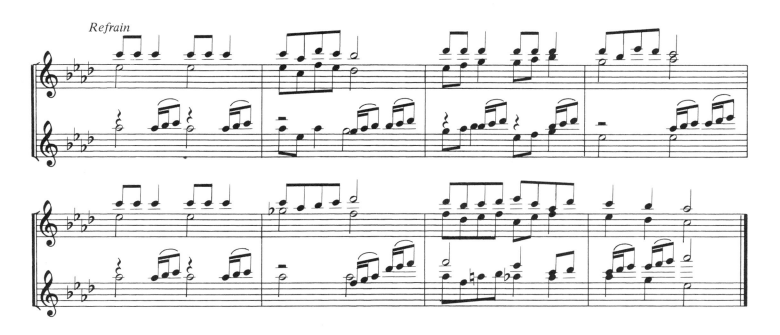

407 'Tis So Sweet to Trust in Jesus

William J. Kirkpatrick

408 He Ransomed Me

J. W. Henderson

1st Violin

2nd Violin

Flutes

3rd Violin

Refrain

Fine

D.S. al Fine

409 Singing I Go

William J. Kirkpatrick

1st Violin

2nd Violin

Flutes

3rd Violin

Refrain

410   A New Name in Glory

C. Austin Miles

411 Now I Belong to Jesus

Norman J. Clayton

412 I Have Settled the Question

Haldor Lillenas

413 Faith of Our Fathers

Henri F. Hemy
Adapt. by James G. Walton

414 It's Just like His Great Love

Clarence B. Strouse

415 There Is a Name I Love to Hear

William H. Havergal

416 Hidden Peace

L. O. Brown

Refrain

rit.

417 Sweet Peace, the Gift of God's Love

Peter P. Bilhorn

Refrain

418 Wonderful Peace

Haldor Lillenas

419 "Thou Wilt Keep Him in Perfect Peace"

Vivian A. Kretz
Arr. by Floyd W. Hawkins

420 The Peace That Jesus Gives

Haldor Lillenas

421 Wonderful Peace

W. G. Cooper

422 Joy Unspeakable

B. E. Warren

423 Sunlight, Sunlight

Winfield S. Weeden

424 Heaven Came Down

John W. Peterson

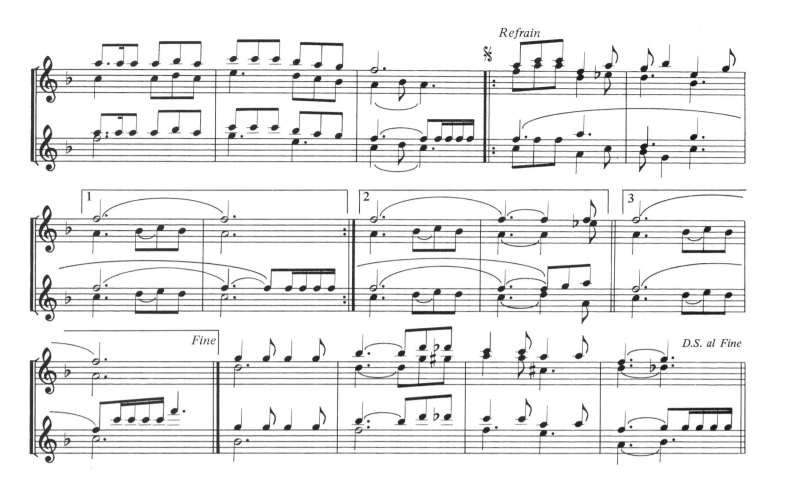

425   The King of Love My Shepherd Is

John B. Dykes

426 Ring the Bells of Heaven

George F. Root

427 In My Heart There Rings a Melody

Elton M. Roth

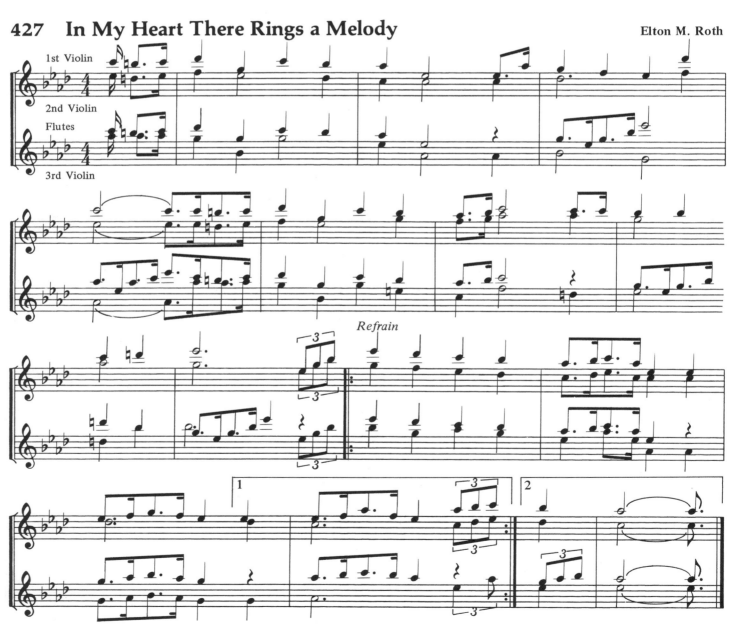

428 Sunshine in My Soul

John R. Sweney

429 You May Have the Joy-bells

William J. Kirkpatrick

430 Glorious Freedom

Alfred Judson

431 Victory All the Time

Lelia N. Morris

432 My Anchor Holds

Daniel B. Towner

433 I Would Not Be Denied

Charles P. Jones

434 Victory in Jesus

Eugene M. Bartlett

435 Jesus Never Fails

Arthur A. Luther

436 Yield Not to Temptation

Horatio R. Palmer

437 Blessed Assurance

Phoebe Palmer Knapp

438 He Giveth More Grace

Hubert Mitchell

439 Have You Any Room for Jesus?

C. C. Williams

440 We Have an Anchor

William J. Kirkpatrick

441 I Know God's Promise Is True

Lelia N. Morris

442 Jesus Is All I Need

Adger M. Pace

443 He Never Has Failed Me Yet

W. J. Henry

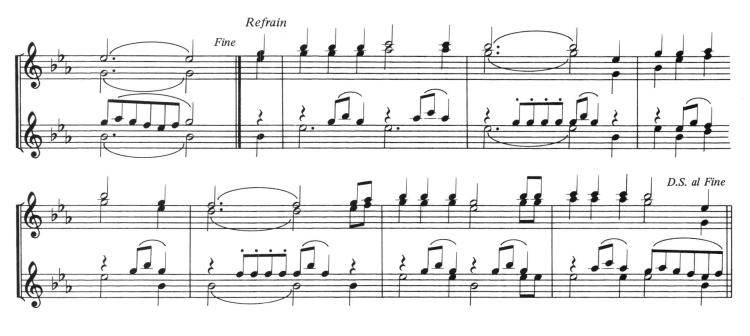

444 His Yoke Is Easy

Ralph E. Hudson

445 O for a Faith That Will Not Shrink

Carl G. Glazer

446 Leaning on the Everlasting Arms

Anthony J. Showalter

447 Yesterday, Today, Forever

J. H. Burke

448 From Every Stormy Wind

Thomas Hastings

1st Violin

2nd Violin

Flutes

3rd Violin

449 I Know Whom I Have Believed

James McGranahan

1st Violin

2nd Violin

Flutes

3rd Violin

Refrain

Div.

450 God Will Take Care of You   W. Stillman Martin

451 Under His Wings   Ira D. Sankey

452 Hiding in Thee

Ira D. Sankey

453 Come, Ye Disconsolate

Samuel Webbe

454 Now the Day Is Over

Joseph Barnby

455 In the Hour of Trial

Spencer Lane

456 Does Jesus Care?

J. Lincoln Hall

457 Trusting Jesus

Ira D. Sankey

458 The Rock That Is Higher than I

William G. Fischer

459 Just When I Need Him Most

Charles H. Gabriel

460 No One Understands like Jesus

John W. Peterson

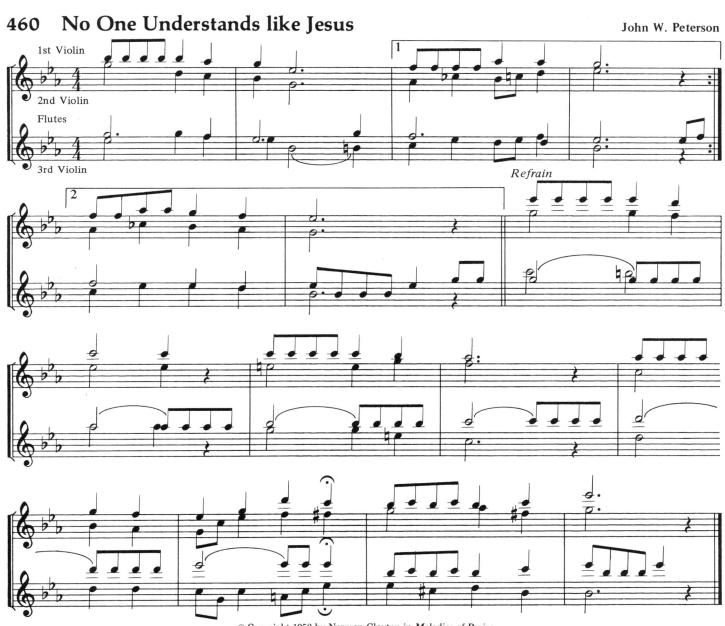

461 Sweetly Resting

W. Warren Bently

462 The Haven of Rest

George D. Moore

463   God Be with You

William G. Tomer

464 No, Not One!

George C. Hugg

465 Trust and Obey

Daniel B. Towner

466 Faith Is the Victory

Ira D. Sankey

467 I Would Be True

Joseph Yates Peek

468 Living by Faith

J. L. Heath

469 I Must Tell Jesus

Elisha A. Hoffman

470 I Need Jesus

Charles H. Gabriel

471 Near to the Heart of God

Cleland B. McAfee

472 Standing on the Promises

R. Kelso Carter

473 Blessed Hour of Prayer

William H. Doane

1st Violin

2nd Violin
Flutes

3rd Violin

474 Tell It to Jesus

Edmund S. Lorenz

1st Violin

2nd Violin
Flutes

3rd Violin

475 Sweet Hour of Prayer

William B. Bradbury

476 I Need Thee Every Hour

Robert Lowry

477 Not My Will, but Thine

Hugh C. Benner

478 Saviour, More than Life

William H. Doane

479 Did You Think to Pray?

William O. Perkins

480 God Leads Us Along

G. A. Young

481 It Is Glory Just to Walk with Him

Haldor Lillenas

482 Jesus, Saviour, Pilot Me

John E. Gould

483 Moment by Moment

May Whittle Moody

484 He Leadeth Me

William B. Bradbury

485 Surely Goodness and Mercy

John W. Peterson

486 The Lord's My Shepherd

Jessie Seymour Irvine

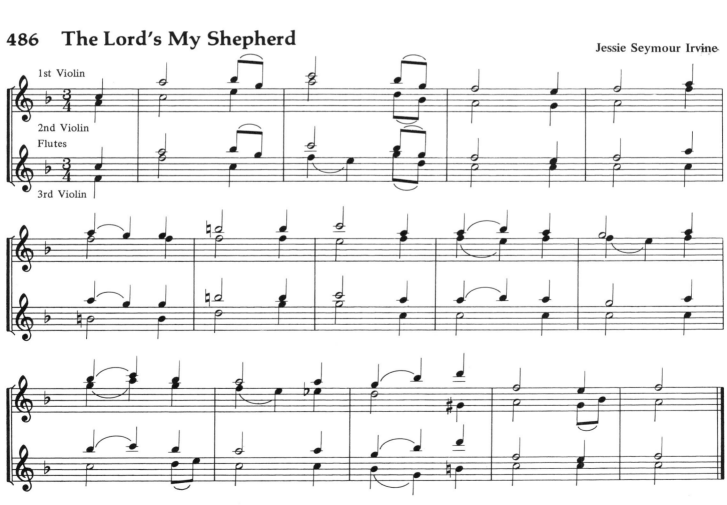

487 The Lord Is My Shepherd

Thomas Koschat

488 Jesus Will Walk with Me

Haldor Lillenas

489 Saviour, like a Shepherd Lead Us

William B. Bradbury

490 All the Way My Saviour Leads

Robert Lowry

491 Lead, Kindly Light

John B. Dykes

492   Jesus Loves Even Me

Philip P. Bliss

495 Our Friendly Church

Hugh C. Benner

496 Praise Him, All Ye Little Children

Anonymous

497 Jesus Loves Me

William B. Bradbury

498 Happy the Home When God Is There

John B. Dykes

499 A Christian Home

Jean Sibelius

1st Violin
2nd Violin
Flutes
3rd Violin

500 O Perfect Love

Joseph Barnby

1st Violin
2nd Violin
Flutes
3rd Violin

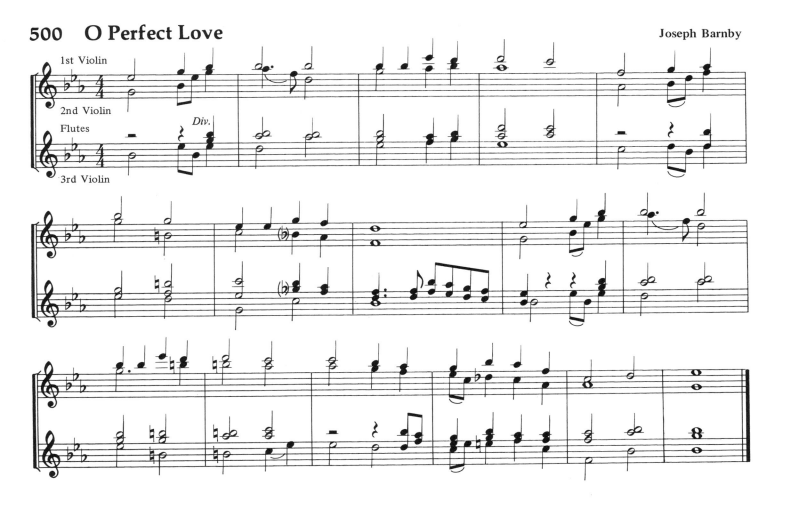

501 The Star-spangled Banner

John Stafford Smith

502 My Country, 'Tis of Thee

Henry Carey

503 O Canada!

Calixa Lavallee

504 God Save the Queen*

Henry Carey

*No. 502 may be used in key of F.

505 America, the Beautiful

Samuel A. Ward

506 Mine Eyes Have Seen the Glory

John William Steffe

507 Let the Beauty of the Lord

Floyd Hawkins

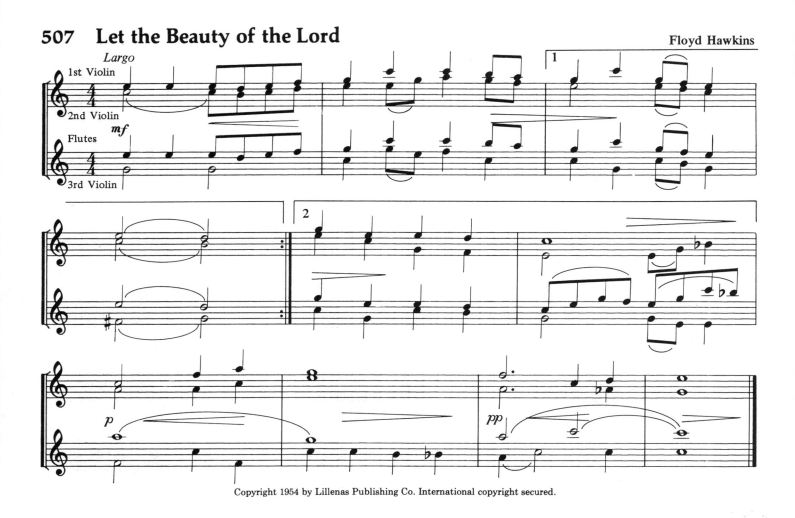

508 Hear Our Prayer, O Lord

George Whelpton

509   Saviour, Again to Thy Dear Name

Edward J. Hopkins

510   The Lord Bless You and Keep You

Peter C. Lutkin

511 Glory Be to the Father

Charles Meineke

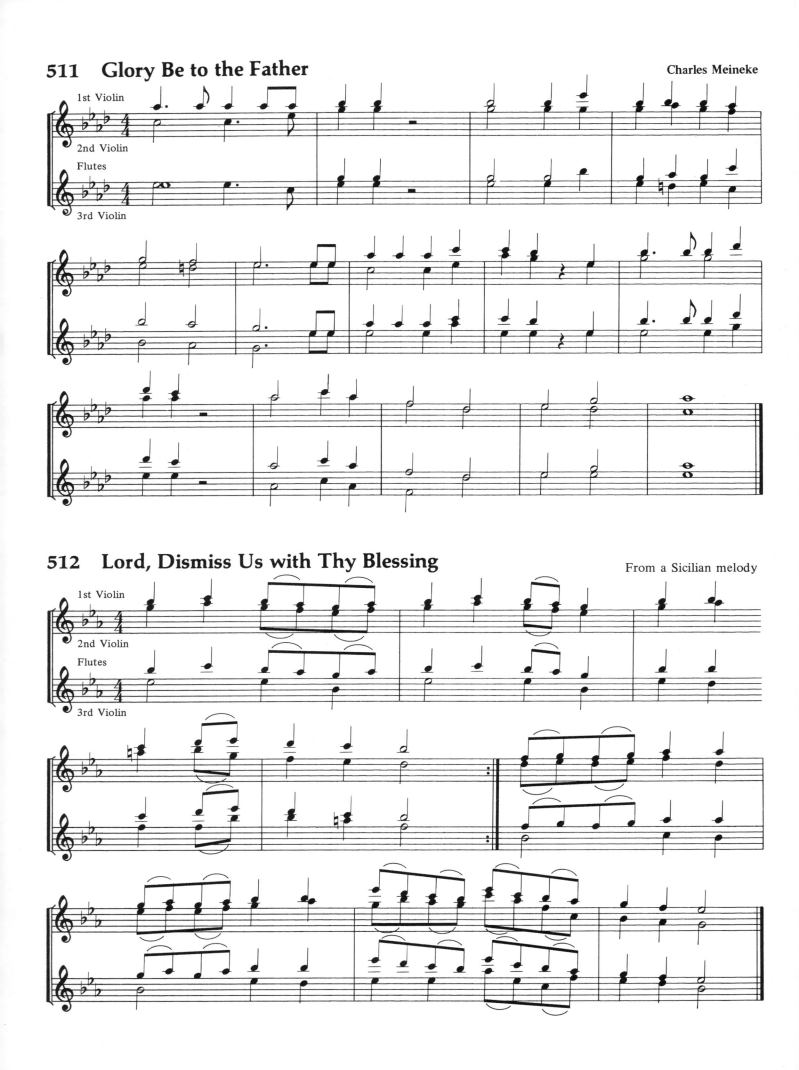

512 Lord, Dismiss Us with Thy Blessing

From a Sicilian melody

513 Praise God, from Whom All Blessings Flow

Louis Bourgeois

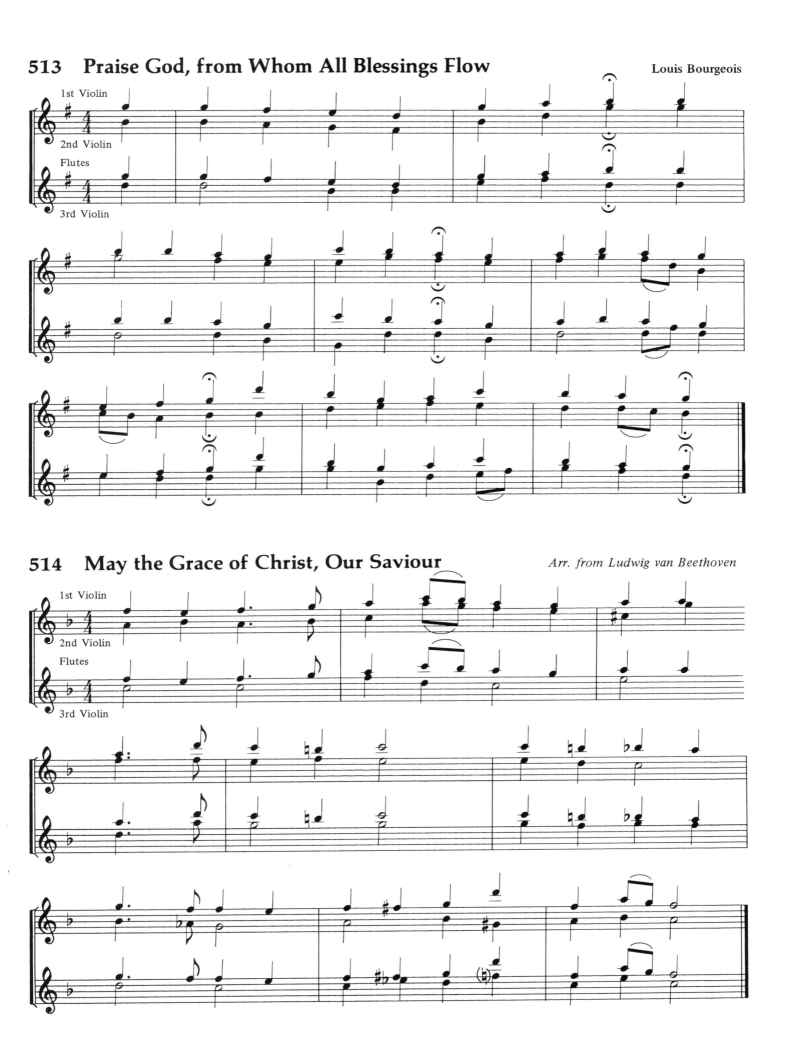

514 May the Grace of Christ, Our Saviour

Arr. from Ludwig van Beethoven

Index